UNSUNG HEROES, SAVING SAIGON

BRIGADIER GENERAL
ALBIN F. IRZYK (RET.)

www.ivyhousebooks.com

PUBLISHED BY IVY HOUSE PUBLISHING GROUP
5122 Bur Oak Circle, Raleigh, NC 27612
United States of America
919-782-0281
www.ivyhousebooks.com

ISBN13: 978-1-57197-488-4
Library of Congress Control Number: 2007908556

Printed in the United States of America

This book is most affectionately dedicated to Evelyn, who has stood with me steadfastly and lovingly for over sixty-one extremely momentous years. Now she is supporting me fully, and has been forfeiting golden evening hours of companionship to help me "get this message out."

A special word of deep and sincere appreciation to my son, Al. He provided me with an invaluable "assist" by giving my manuscript a thorough going over, which vastly improved it.

Also by Brigadier General Albin F. Irzyk (Ret.)

He Rode Up Front for Patton

Gasoline to Patton, A Different War

The 14th Armored Calvary Regiment During the Berlin Crisis 1961

CONTENTS

PREFACE

Our society continually comes up with unsung heroes. There are unsung heroes in communities, government, academia, medicine, sports. Yes, there are even unsung heroes in the military. This is the story of such an unsung hero—an Army command in Vietnam—more specifically, United States Army Headquarters Area Command, or USAHAC, or more simply—HAC.

In time many unsung heroes are recognized—receive awards, trophies, plaques, and write-ups in newspapers and magazines. This recognition is richly deserved. However, when this happens, when people recognize and publicize what those heroes have done—sing their praises—in a sense they are no longer *unsung* heroes.

This story is about the unlikeliest of heroes—a pure, literal, unsung hero. It's accomplishments and achievements have remained totally unrecognized and unappreciated, since January and early February of 1968.

There have been hundreds of books and millions of words written about the U.S. involvement in Vietnam—many thousands of words about Saigon during TET of 1968. Yet, to this day, there has not been a single mention in any publication about the role that HAC played in that battle. Thus, in the absolute, truest sense—it remains *unsung*.

Historians appear to be unaware of, or have ignored, the vital, critical role played by this tiny, obscure unit in that city. It is, undoubtedly, the unit's small size and its unusual and little-understood mission that has invited that obscurity.

It is universally recognized that the most significant military effort during the Vietnam War was the totally unexpected, inconceivable, and shocking North Vietnamese offensive launched during TET of 1968. The TET offensive was such a dominant effort, and had such a decisive effect, that it proved to be the turning point of that war.

The North Vietnamese offensive focused on many specific objectives. But without question the one at the very top of the list was seizing control of Saigon, the capital city of South Vietnam. It was not only a very juicy military target; there was no question that its seizure would have boundless, earth-shaking, worldwide psychological repercussions. It was by far the choicest target of all.

In many places and many respects the NVA TET offensive fell well short of the expectations of the high command. But their greatest failure by far was their inability to gain quickly their prime objective—the seizure of Saigon.

It is true that their plan for Saigon had faults. In its execution there was lack of proper coordination, and there were lapses of professionalism. Nevertheless, their plans could have worked, their mission could have been accomplished, Saigon could have been seized had it not been for the totally unexpected and unpredicted interference by our tiny, pesky unsung hero. That command early on played a fantastic, unbelievably pivotal role.

As we know so well, individuals often become heroes because of the positive, immediate way in which they respond to and react in emergency situations—situations that are suddenly thrust upon them—situations that they never expected and for which they were totally unprepared.

An explosion occurs, a fire ensues, people are injured, begin to panic. An individual steps forth, takes control, and brings order out of chaos. A hero is born, but he moves on before he is known, and becomes an unsung hero.

An individual out for an innocent stroll hears cries for help. He dives fully clothed into the river, and rescues a terrified, drowning teenager. As the ambulance moves on, so does the rescuer—another unsung hero.

And so it was with HAC. When the surprising attack on Saigon was launched during the early hours of 31 January 1968, that command had thrust upon it a series of challenges to astonishing events—events which were absolutely unbelievable, which in the wildest of imaginings could not have been envisioned—events for which it had never been organized, trained, equipped, manned, or prepared. It was confronted with a super emergency. Its response, particularly during the absolutely crucial early hours, was immediate and heroic. Those actions were a critical factor in the saving of Saigon—in preventing the enemy from taking early control of South Vietnam's capital city.

No Hollywood scriptwriter would have dreamed of fashioning that particular unit for that particular scenario. Here was a small, little known, little understood organization that performed absolutely extraordinarily.

During those momentous hours, I was the Commanding General of HAC. I am greatly puzzled—yes, dismayed—that the valiant and successful efforts of my command continue to remain completely unrecognized. There is a gap, a void—admittedly a very small one, when one considers the totality of our multi-year involvement in Vietnam, but a void, nevertheless—in the reporting of and the historical accounts of that war, particularly the battle for Saigon.

My purpose here is to bridge that gap and fill that void. I recognize all too well that "time has marched on." Our citizenry by and large became very jaded by the Vietnam War. At this late stage they are well beyond that, and have had their fill and then some. The last thing they want are more words about that conflict. Yet I feel a very strong obligation, even at this very late stage, to tell the HAC story.

I ask, "If not I, who?" If I do not do it, it will not be done and a very valuable bit of history will be lost. The years ahead for me are rapidly diminishing, I am in my ninety-first year, and if it is to be done, I cannot delay much longer.

On behalf of all the individuals who served so heroically, valiantly, and selflessly under the HAC banner, as HAC's Commander, I believe that it is vitally important—that it is my duty—to "sing" about HAC, and to remove the "un" from *unsung*. That command has rested in obscurity for far too long.

So, the prime purpose of the words that follow is simply to put HAC's heroic, selfless performance "on the record." Thus it will be available to the students of history, and to the curious during the decades ahead.

I came bolt upright in my bed. Loud, booming, reverberating explosions had abruptly and rudely awakened me. I jumped out of bed, glanced at my watch, and furiously began dressing in the clothes I laid out each night for just such an emergency. My watch read 2:47 A.M. The noise was close—very close—not more than five or six blocks from me in downtown Saigon. Something *big*, something very critical was happening.

I dashed out the door. Fast as I had been, Sergeant Williams was faster. My six-foot-five-inch Military Police driver and bodyguard was standing fully dressed with the car doors open and the engine idling. Without a word we both jumped in, and the car was moving in reverse, heading out the driveway, as we slammed the doors shut.

Once on the street we turned and headed for my headquarters. One glance told me that something was wrong, terribly wrong. My first thought was, "What has happened to all the people?"

When I had slipped into bed just a few hours earlier, the streets were jammed, a teeming mass of humanity. Pedicabs, taxis, and cars were stopped cold, barely able to move. Even individuals were having difficulty pushing their way along. The city was celebrating the Lunar New Year, and this night had been the peak of the celebration. Everyone was a reveler—singing, dancing, laughing, shouting, screaming. Everywhere firecrackers were popping, snapping, bouncing in endless strings.

Now, as the car picked up speed, unbelievably the streets were deathly still. Not a single soul of Saigon's three million was visible. No one. Not one light was showing. It was eerie, uncanny, breathtaking. The sudden, remarkable contrast was unimaginable. It was as though a plague had hit the city, and wiped it out in one fell swoop.

General Westmoreland had called me hours before, and told me to have my command at full alert, as he had information that there might be sappers operating in the city that night. Now it was perfectly obvious that whoever or whatever was in Saigon this night was far more and much bigger than mere sappers. My car was not moving at the usual slow, tortuous pace, but amazingly it was racing along the Saigon streets at sixty miles per hour—yes, sixty miles per hour. In Saigon's long history it is safe to say that no car had ever traversed its streets at such speed and never would again.

Ah, but there was life out there, somewhere, in the darkness. Scattered, random rifle shots—definitely not firecrackers—were aimed at my speeding car, but fell harmlessly behind.

After what normally was a time consuming trip, but now seemed but an instant, the car slowed as it approached a large sign that read UNITED STATES ARMY HEADQUARTERS AREA COMMAND—my headquarters.

The security guard recognized my car, opened the gate, and waved me through. I rushed into the building, raced up the stairs into the Duty Officer's room. Chaos. Pandemonium. He and his augmented staff were frantic. Every phone within sight and sound was ringing incessantly, demanding to be answered. There were not enough hands, arms and ears.

The minute he noted my presence, the duty officer rushed up to me. His first words were, "Sir, our Embassy is under attack. Our MPs have been dispatched, and are rushing to it."

The 1968 TET attack on Saigon was furiously unfolding.

SETTING THE STAGE

CHAPTER 1
WHAT IS TET?

TET. A three-letter word. But a word that has appeared hundreds of thousands of times in newspapers, magazines, articles, stories, and books. A word that has glibly passed the lips of many thousands of people.

Most know and associate it with a remarkable event, the turning point of the Vietnam War. Those who wish to understand the meaning of the word learn that it is the Chinese-Vietnamese Lunar New Year. That knowledge seems to satisfy most, and they probe no further.

Only when one understands the magnitude of TET in the lives and culture of the Vietnamese people, and realizes that its origin dates back to the years before Christ, can he comprehend and fully appreciate the totally unbelievable surprise that the North Vietnamese military forces achieved when they launched their nationwide offensive during the early hours of January 31, 1968—TET, the Year of the Monkey.

Those actions at that specific time were unbelievable, incomprehensible, and that they were actually taking place evoked amazement, consternation, shock, incredulity, and disbelief.

To understand the "why" of those emotions, one must know what TET is.

This is what TET is.

TET is the Chinese New Year. It is the most important holiday celebrated by Asians around the world.

The Chinese New Year always falls on the first new moon after the sun has left the sign of Capricorn and entered Aquarius—from January 21 to February 19. But instead of zodiac signs, the Chinese call the year by its animal name.

It has been said that Buddha called to him all the animals in the kingdom. Only twelve appeared—the rat, ox, tiger, hare, dragon, serpent, horse, sheep, monkey, rooster, dog, and boar. Buddha named the calendar years in their honor, and in the order in which they came.

The twelve months of the Chinese calendar contain only twenty-nine or thirty days each. As the total does not add up to the 365 days in the solar year, a double month is added every thirty months, or three and a half years.

TET was first observed in Vietnam when it was under Chinese domination. Though no specific date is recorded of the first observance of TET in Vietnam, it probably began around 200 BC, during the long period of domination by the Chinese. The rites that accompany Vietnamese TET, however, have changed during the ages, and now show only a remote resemblance to the original Chinese festival.

For the Vietnamese, as it has been with the Chinese, it is the most important holiday of the year. It is far more than celebrating the start of a new year. It is like combining our Christmas, New Year's, Easter, and the Fourth of July into a single holiday. That makes it a "whopper" of a festival, and a complicated one as well. It incorporates the hoopla and pageantry of the Fourth of July with the brotherhood and cheer of Christmas, the nostalgia and optimism of New Year's Eve, with the quiet joy and introspection of Easter. TET, however, lasts for three days.

And if that is not enough, there is added significance to the day. TET not only heralds the advent of the New Year, but the beginning of spring. It is also a birthday. Unlike Western countries, the Vietnamese do not celebrate each individual birthday. Everyone, no matter where or when he was born, is a year older at TET. If an individual is born today, and the next day is TET, he is already two years old.

It is a time of general rejoicing—a combination of solemnity, gaiety, and hope—a time when all get a new start. As in spring, when the trees adorn themselves with new buds after losing their dry and dead leaves, so men and women throw aside their worries, their past mistakes, their hatreds, and their grief

It is a time to pay homage to ancestors, visit family and friends, observe traditional taboos, and, of course, to celebrate. This is the last chance to correct faults, pardon others for their offenses, to have enemies become friends, and to pay debts. To be a debtor during TET is a sign of bad luck, since what happens during TET determines what the new year will bring. This is the time when the Vietnamese people look back on the past, enjoy the present, and look forward to the future.

At the beginning of TET, it is believed that ancestors return to the world. Families invite all the deceased relatives to their homes to share and enjoy the festivities with them. Special foods are prepared for the ancestors and placed on family altars, and special prayers are said to them. At midnight on the last day of the old year, food and flowers are offered to the ancestors. On the fourth day, the ancestors return to their heavenly abodes, and people visit graves to serve as escorts for their departure.

Traditionally, three days of activities precede the Lunar New Year. On the first day, families go to their parents' house, or to a superior relative (if the parents are deceased) to offer a New Year's wish.

Children are instructed to behave, not to do anything wrong, not to utter any bad words, because on New Year's Day, if they misbehave, say things they should not, or get into a fight, they will be in trouble for a whole year.

On the second day preceding the new year, families visit the homes of friends. Visitors during TET traditionally bring gifts for the family. The wife may be given a bouquet of red flowers. Gifts for adults, however, are less important than for children. The youngsters are given a small red basket and money wrapped in red-colored paper. The red color is the lucky color. Stamped on the outside of the wrapper is *phuc,* the symbol of happiness. Since New Year's Day is everyone's birthday, the gift of money is a special gift with special meaning. Some gifts are taboo such as medicines and vitamins, sharp objects, or anything not new.

The evening of the third day is a time reserved for the remembrance of ancestors. After much celebrating has been done and a final farewell dinner consumed, votive papers, representing money, are burned. This is a symbolic payment for the sampan that ferries the ancestors across the river between heaven and earth. They have celebrated the end of the year, "Tat Nun," a year finished.

Visiting is an important part of TET, but so is the eating, the feasting. In traditionally good and gracious style, the Vietnamese women prepare feasts and make decorations. The feasts include many special foods. No New Year's is complete without *banh* day and *banh chung* cakes. Each cake—one round, representing the heavens, the other square, a symbol of earth—represents the balanced opposites in the world. These cakes are served only at TET.

The decorations also represent balanced opposites, based on Taoist religious symbols. Brightly colored vertical banners inscribed with ancient Chinese characters traditionally hang opposite each other, each sentence constructed of opposites—like black and white. If one phrase says earth, the other must say sky.

Additional cooked delicacies include chicken baked in pepper sauce, traditional rice cakes wrapped in banana leaves, fish and pork rolls, and a special delicacy for the TET holiday only—the shrimp-filled egg roll.

Other interesting and significant highlights concerning TET:

a. Traditionally, prime importance is attached to the first visitor during Tet. The Vietnamese believe that he influences the fortunes of the family for the rest of the year. A pleasant and prosperous first visitor brings happiness and good fortune, while a sad and discourteous one brings hardship and ill fortune during the next twelve months. Should a rich man visit first, the family's fortunes will surely improve. Many families plan well ahead, leaving no room for chance.

So in very many cases the first person to visit a family has already been selected by that family.

b. Individuals adorn themselves in all new, brightly colored clothes, especially yellow and red—the good luck colors. Anyone who goes out on the first day of TET wearing old clothing is admitting to the lowest form of poverty.

c. They sing age-old songs—the New Year's Eve song, "Ly Ruou Mung," and their national anthem, "Viet Nam, Viet Nam."

d. TET is not only a time for spiritual rededication, but a period of fun and excitement as well. Thrift is temporarily forgotten, and large quantities of food, clothing, candles, and flowers are purchased for the holidays. Best wishes for the new year are offered by everyone. Homes are gaily decorated, and warm hospitality is extended to all visitors.

e. TET is also a time for firecrackers. The popping of firecrackers is widespread. Everyone engages in it. The Vietnamese say that firecrackers are the ambassadors of spring; they announce a good beginning on the first day of the New Year. However, the motivation behind exploding firecrackers seemed to be to make as much noise and to create as much excitement and enjoyment as possible. The tradition of firecrackers at TET is derived from legend. Originally, the Vietnamese exploded firecrackers to frighten away evil spirits. The noise and light of firecrackers served to keep the evil spirits at a safe distance, until the return of the benevolent spirits who were away paying their respects to the Emperor of Jade in heaven.

f. The Vietnamese, like all peoples, have superstitions and taboos. Some of these taboos, however, apply only during TET. It is considered bad luck, for example, to insult others, show grief, or break dishes. The Vietnamese will go to great lengths to prevent or avoid arguments, violent emotions, or insults. Also, it is bad luck to clean house. The legend behind this taboo relates that a wealthy merchant and his beautiful concubine quarreled on the first day of TET because she dropped a curio that broke. After he had scolded and beaten her, she hid in a pile of refuse. The merchant, not knowing the girl was hiding there, had the pile thrown outside. The girl disappeared, and from that time on, his fortune slipped away until it was lost. To avoid sweeping away any fortune brought by the New Year, homes are not swept during the three days of TET.

g. Employers give their employees bonuses at this time of year

h. According to legend, on the twenty-third day of the last month of the year, the good spirits go to heaven for seven days to report to the Jade Emperor on the year's events. The Jade Emperor uses this information to determine the family's fortunes for the coming year. Conversely, while the good spirits are going to heaven, evil spirits are released from hell, also for seven days. The Vietnamese go to great lengths and utilize many superstitious symbols as a means of protecting themselves from those evil spirits.

i. Finally, and most importantly, every Vietnamese individual, regardless of who he is, what he is, and where he is, wants to be home with his own family for the holiday.

So there you have it. That is TET. No matter from what angle, vantage point, or perspective it is viewed, one must agree that for the Vietnamese it is not only a big, huge holiday—it is monumental.

The North Vietnamese knew this well. As individuals, they had grown up obeying, applying, glorying in their culture, and following its customs, traditions, taboos. It was ingrained in them.

They knew that at TET the whole populace would be celebrating, worshipping and partying.

They knew that at no other time during the year was the country's "guard down," and was as vulnerable as it was at TET.

They knew full well that in keeping with tradition, military authorities would free every possible individual—leaving military units significantly undermanned—so that they could be home with their families.

They knew without question or doubt that they would surprise, and they anticipated that the surprise would be so stunning that it would lead to widespread victory.

It obviously did not matter to them that they turned their backs, thumbed their noses at century old traditions—things that they had been raised with, and taught to believe in so deeply and so strongly.

Yes, it worked. Their surprise, nationwide offensive to coincide with the TET holiday turned out to be a crowning psychological achievement.

Theirs was a "no holds barred" philosophy. Their actions, at the very least, were blasphemous.

Since this was now all-out war, conscience no longer mattered. However, if they did need something to help them rationalize, to excuse their behavior and their actions, there was a historic precedent that they could fall back upon. In 1789 Vietnamese patriots had attacked the occupying Chinese during the Lunar New Year festival. Yet, even with that precedent they would be straining mightily, for in 1789 it was the Vietnamese against the Chinese, whereas in the 1968 TET, it was brother versus brother, Vietnamese against Vietnamese.

SETTING THE STAGE

CHAPTER 2
WHAT WAS SAIGON?

It was 1954. I was ordered to Hawaii, and joined the staff of CINCPAC (Commander in Chief, Pacific, Admiral Felix B. Stump). CINCPAC was a joint staff, and included personnel from the Navy, Army, Air Force, and Marines.

1954 turned out to be an important, significant, memorable, and historic year for Southeast Asia, and particularly Vietnam. And I was privileged to occupy a seat on the fifty-yard line.

Just two months before I assumed my duties at CINCPAC, the French-Indochina War ended. The final chapter of that war was written with the fall, after a long siege, of the French garrison at Dien Bien Phu. That ended what had long been French domination and control of the area.

To better understand the significance of those events, it is appropriate that we briefly examine the past and follow the steps that brought it to 1954.

For a long period of time Vietnam was part of the kingdom of Cambodia. The Vietnamese first gained entry into the region in the seventeenth century. Relations with the French began in the eighteenth century, when French traders and missionaries settled in the area.

The important town of Saigon, which rested less than fifty miles from the South China Sea, was captured by the French in 1859. At that time there were fewer than fifteen thousand people residing in

Saigon. In 1862 the town was ceded to the French by the Vietnamese Emperor, Tu Duc.

Under the French, the town was transformed into a major port. Additionally, the French brought to it their culture and mores. As the years passed, Saigon was developed into a place of beautiful villas, imposing public buildings, and well-paved, tree-lined boulevards. By 1936 the population had increased to 111,000, of which approximately 11,760 were French.

Then came World War II. Saigon was occupied by the Japanese in 1940. However, French colonial authorities were permitted to administer Vietnam until 1945. After the Japanese surrender of that year, Vietnamese independence was declared. However, it was very short-lived. Celebrations in Saigon turned into a riot. French troops seized control of the city, and thus began the French-Indochina War that would last for nine years.

The day after the fall of the French garrison at Dien Bien Phu, May 8, 1954, negotiations immediately began. Agreements were finally signed on July 21 between the French and Vietnamese, as well as the Laotian and Cambodian representatives. These proceedings would be referred to as the Geneva Conference, and the agreements as the Geneva Accords.

The main provision of these agreements was a ceasefire along the 17th parallel. This effectively divided Vietnam into northern and southern zones. Hanoi, of course, was the capital of North Vietnam, while Saigon became the capital of South Vietnam.

North Vietnam was Communist. The United States lent its support, and endeavored to help build a separate, democratic state in South Vietnam.

Seeing the handwriting on the wall, vast numbers of individuals, using great ingenuity and every means imaginable, fled from the Communism of North Vietnam to the fledgling democracy in the South. Most headed for Saigon. Absorbing the unexpected flood of humanity proved difficult, and posed a real challenge for the city. The cultural and political life of Saigon was complicated but enriched by the influx from North Vietnam.

Another important development occurred a short time later. United States Secretary of State, John Foster Dulles, had long recognized the strategic importance of Southeast Asia, and decided to take appropriate action. In this he was supported by President Dwight D. Eisenhower. Secretary Dulles then spearheaded an effort that truly became his "baby." His efforts came to fruition in September of 1954 when the Southeast Asia Collective Defense Treaty (SEACDT), on occasion referred to as the Manila Pact, was born in Manila, the Philippines. It soon became known as SEATO (Southeast Asia Treaty Organization). Eight nations that had interests in the area became members of the organization and signatories of the treaty. These were Australia, New Zealand, Pakistan, France, the Philippines, Thailand, Great Britain, and the United States.

Most interestingly, by a special protocol the eight member nations unanimously agreed to apply the protective provisions of the treaty to three other countries. These three nations, which were not SEATO members, covered critical areas in Southeast Asia, and were known as the Protocol States. They were Laos, Cambodia, and South Vietnam.

SEATO was a regional, international organization. It was the first multinational treaty entered into by the United States in that part of the world.

Admiral Stump attended the meeting in Manila. Shortly, in addition to his other duties and responsibilities, he was designated as the U.S. Military Advisor to SEATO. That meant that he would represent the U.S. on all military matters discussed or decided upon. Ironically, although an organization like NATO, then and now, has been universally known, very few in America and elsewhere have ever been aware of the existence of SEATO. It had absolutely no impact on the Vietnam War, and faded out of existence without ever being truly effective.

During the many years of the Vietnam War, members of SEATO such as New Zealand, Australia, and the Philippines provided token forces, and Thailand was helpful. But, ironically, it was a non-SEATO nation that provided an extensive military presence in support of the

U.S. South Korea provided forces that consisted of at least two divisions and a corps headquarters.

In the fall of 1954 there was still another development. Admiral Stump, in addition to having command of all U.S. military forces in the Pacific area, and recently being designated as U.S. Military Advisor to SEATO, was given direct command of the military assistance advisory groups in his area. These included groups located in Taiwan, the Philippines, Thailand, Cambodia, and South Vietnam.

To keep pace with our commander, we on his staff also had multiple responsibilities. We did our primary job of military planning for the Pacific command area. We, as U.S. delegates, attended numerous SEATO conferences in Southeast Asia, and as our commander's eyes and ears, we paid staff visits to the military assistance advisory groups under his command.

It was Admiral Stump's additional responsibilities that enabled me to pay my first visit to South Vietnam and its capital of Saigon. During my months at CINCPAC, I had heard much about Saigon. It had some most intriguing references. I had heard it called "Paris of the East" and "Pearl of the Orient." From what I had read and heard, it was an interesting, even fascinating, city. Adjectives like "exotic" had been used to describe it. So I became quite excited when I learned that I, finally, would be visiting Saigon. I immediately began looking forward to that visit with keen anticipation and great expectations.

I arrived for my first look at Saigon in January of 1956. The purpose of my staff visit was to examine the operation of JUSMAAG (Joint U.S. Military Assistance Advisory Group), Vietnam. At that time the JUSMAAG was the main U.S. presence in South Vietnam, with its headquarters in Saigon. I was sent by my headquarters to take a good look at what they were doing, to ascertain that they were, indeed, successfully performing their assigned mission.

Since my headquarters was also theirs, and since it is understandable that they would want to look good in the eyes of the representative from that headquarters, I was certain that I would be well received, and shown every kindness and courtesy that they could extend, and I was not disappointed.

My plane was met, and I was immediately driven to the heart of Saigon and to my hotel. It was called the Caravelle. As I got out of the car, I could not help but notice across a very broad street or square another hotel, the Continental Palace. One glance told me that these two hotels were probably the best in the city. This proved to be the case. The Caravelle appeared to be the newer of the two, but the Continental Palace seemed more sedate, had more atmosphere with an established old world charm. It had broad verandas with tables and chairs. My first glance in that direction noted that most of those were occupied with guests enjoying drinks and afternoon snacks.

My hosts knew that this was my first visit to Saigon. So as soon as I registered and while it was still daylight, they suggested a quick tour of the city. I was most eager to get started.

When we returned to the hotel, I readily conceded that although I had expected much, the city more than lived up to my fondest expectations.

I found it to be a beautiful, imposing city. It had broad, tree-lined (many with double rows of trees), very impressive boulevards. There were large, imposing, old French villas, fashionable boutiques, cafes. It was a city of fountains, statues, public gardens. The French influence and features were obvious, everywhere. Buildings like the Government House, law courts, theaters, and the cathedral were distinctly French. After traversing the city, I could readily and easily understand the appellation, "Little Paris of the East."

There were moments during my tour when I actually believed that I was somewhere in France. Saigon reminded me strongly of a large provincial city in that country. I could easily visualize that it could have been picked up, lifted, and transported to such a locality as Lorraine, and placed not too far from Nancy.

There were many similarities to the French, but there were also marked differences that made Saigon a city unique unto itself. Although the backdrop of buildings, fountains, and boulevards was very much like France, life on the streets was distinctively Vietnamese. Although France, for example, had an abundance of bicycles, in Saigon they were out in vastly greater numbers.

No city in France had the wide variety of transportation that was found on the streets of Saigon. In Nancy, for example, one would never see a common conveyance that appeared to be a wide, wicker seat propelled from behind by a man with powerfully built legs and knotted calves, wearing a conical straw hat and riding what can best be described as the front half of a bicycle.

In Nancy one would not see what in Saigon was seen everywhere. It was the common, universal female attire, the *ao dai.* This was an ankle length, flowing costume that was sharply slit up the side, almost to the hip.

So, yes, Saigon evidenced considerable French influence, but the city now was Vietnamese, and had its own distinctive, unique customs and culture.

The city that I visited was laid back, unhurried. It had apparently absorbed the influx of refugees from the North, for the sidewalks and broad boulevards were not the least bit crowded, and easily accommodated the wide variety of traffic.

Life moved along at a slow, leisurely, serene, unruffled pace. At times this pace seemed languid, almost lazy. Because of the heat, life seemed to stop during the middle of the day. People disappeared to get into the shade, and to rest or nap. It appeared that only the Americans were active during the middle of the day.

Later in the afternoon after the heat became less oppressive, and as though a switch was flicked, out of the woodwork came the populace. There was almost instant activity, everywhere. Shops, cafes, and restaurants filled quickly with afternoon patrons. This daily routine, consequently, pushed back the dinner hour—much later than we Americans were accustomed to. For the American military, whose day began very early, these late hours at times could become awkward and taxing.

What was impressive and noteworthy was the service experienced everywhere in Saigon. It can best be described as impeccable, and there was plenty of it. In the hotels, which were most efficiently operated, white-jacketed young men were everywhere, ready to assist. They were not only readily available when one had a request, but were constantly asking if they could do this or that for you.

In restaurants such as the Continental Palace the menus were broad, and the food prepared to perfection. We were served not by a waiter, but by a team of waiters. They were clustered unobtrusively nearby. It took only the nodding of a head or a motion of the hand to have them at the table.

What I experienced in Saigon was the "colonial life" of the British and French, which I had read about over the years. But elegance reached a new level for me when I was invited to play tennis at the Cercle Sportif. This was without question the "it" place, the "in" place in Saigon. Here was where the Saigon establishment—the wealthy, the well placed—gathered in a restricted, very elite environment.

The courts themselves were close to perfection. Ball boys were constantly at one's elbow. There was no bending for or retrieving of balls by the players. Then, after the game, exotic drinks were available, as well as mouthwatering choices for lunch. This was "the good life" personified.

That was the Saigon that I experienced in the mid-fifties.

Four years later, in 1960, I was privileged and most fortunate to make an official 'round the world' trip with an Assistant Secretary of the Army. This was a fast-paced, rather hectic journey that included many stops, but, of necessity, each of short duration. One of those stops was Saigon. The visit consisted of a series of briefings immediately after landing, a reception, a late dinner, and early departure. What I saw of Saigon was just a blur. From the few peeks that I had of the city, I concluded that not much had changed since my previous visit.

When I departed that morning, I had no expectations of ever returning. Little did I know then that the future had a return trip in store for me.

Yes, I would be back in Saigon, but this time not for a quick visit.

Rather, unbelievably for me, I would be taking up residence in the city. I would not only live there, but I would learn to know the city intimately, have many responsibilities within the city, and exert considerable influence upon it.

My return to Saigon occurred in the early fall of 1967, a bit over seven years after my previous visit. I had orders to take command of a U.S. Army Headquarters in that city.

Little did I realize that upon landing at Tan Son Nhut I was about to experience one of the great shocks of my life. The moment my feet hit the tarmac, I could sense, see, and feel that this was a changed, radically different city. The airport gave me my first clue. There was everywhere about it a military presence, but it was organized in anything but a military manner. There were clusters and piles of things placed haphazardly in all directions. It had a dirty, disorganized, unkempt, hurried atmosphere.

Once in the car heading for the center of the city, I found the heat typically oppressive. But it seemed more stifling than I had remembered it, and there was now a new, unpleasant, seemingly omnipresent odor.

But the most astonishing spectacle was the traffic. People and vehicles of every imaginable variety and description jammed the sidewalks and streets. This was no longer a lazy, laid back city. It was now a frenzied, frustrated, slow moving mass of humanity.

The car edged its way to my two initial destinations: first, the office in downtown Saigon where I would work, and second, the home, also in downtown Saigon, in which I would reside.

At times the car, as it dragged slowly along, would be forced to come to a complete stop. At some of the main intersections the traffic was so interlocked that I thought it just could not be untangled, and that I might be witnessing what appeared to be the last, great, final traffic jam.

But it, finally, moved again.

As I would learn in the days ahead, the traffic always eventually moved. This might be in fits and starts, but it moved. So I was always, ultimately, able to get to wherever I needed to be. Some days would be better than others, but the only constant was that it was busy and totally unpredictable.

I successfully reached the headquarters of my new command and the office in which I would work. As I sat in the chair behind my desk, my first act was to sign the only piece of paper that rested on the desk. It had the headquarters designation and the date—September 23, 1967—and simply read, "I hereby assume Command." I signed my name to it and at that moment I became the Commanding General of the United States Army Headquarters Area Command, and unofficially, the "military mayor" of Saigon.

I was taken on a quick tour of the headquarters, and was introduced to and met the people with whom I would now be working. The headquarters complex was well inside metropolitan Saigon, but was some distance from the center of the city. My first impression was that the headquarters was jammed into space that could barely accommodate it. There seemed to be little elbowroom. Not too many weeks later the headquarters was able to move into more appropriate facilities, but well out and on the perimeter of the city.

After leaving the headquarters area, I was driven to my residence. It was located close to the center of the city, and was not too many blocks away from such landmarks as the cathedral and the United States Embassy. It was a one-story stone building that had obviously been around for a long time, but was in good condition. It was ideal for a single resident, and had room for small meetings and conferences that I might wish to hold away from the headquarters.

On my day of arrival and during the drive from the airport into the city, I concluded that, "Saigon is a changed city." As the days passed, and as I really got to know the city, I recognized the word "changed" was a gross understatement. In just two handfuls of years Saigon had undergone a radical, unbelievable, revolutionary transformation.

On the day of my arrival in Saigon, I became a resident of the most densely populated city on the face of the earth. This development was absolutely incredible. From a town of fifteen thousand in

1859 to this—in less than one hundred years—was a huge, enormous, gargantuan leap.

As the days passed, I could find no evidence that a government census had been taken at any time during recent years. Consequently, there were no such things as "official" figures. This was perfectly understandable. With the situation existing, as will be described, it would have been impossible for the government to make an accurate, reliable, authentic counting of the teeming masses living in Saigon. Thus reliance had to continue to be made on estimates. And those estimates of the city's population ranged from a low of two million to a more realistic high of three million, or even three million plus.

The residents of Saigon occupied an area of approximately 24.2 square miles. If one took the low estimate of two million, that tallied at seventy thousand human beings per square mile. *Wow!* That is really being jammed into a place. Hong Kong, with less than sixty thousand per square mile, came in at a not-close second. Tokyo, always perceived as a very crowded city, surprisingly lagged well behind with only 44,000 per square mile. And New York, which to most Americans was a very heavily populated city, figured in at thirty thousand, which was less than half of the folks crowded together in Saigon.

There were several factors to explain this enormous population jump. However, there were two main ones. The first was that more and more people from the countryside moved to the city seeking greater economic opportunity. The second, and more important, was the decision, with the war escalating, to flee from the increasingly dangerous countryside to what they perceived to be the relative security and safety that the large city of Saigon could provide.

While twenty years before, only a portion of the population lived in the cities, the estimate now was that at least one-third of Vietnamese citizens were city dwellers. If those figures were accepted, that would mean that fifteen percent of the national population of South Vietnam lived in its capital city.

But the influx was not a help; instead it was a frustrating, exasperating hindrance. Many viewed it as an albatross around the neck of the city.

Saigon had been built up over the years by the French, and was expected when "fully grown" to be able to accommodate about 550,000 people. Now it had four or five times that number or more. The city faced the awesome and imposing task of providing a city's fundamental necessities—water, electric power, sanitation, health facilities, housing, and other required municipal services—to this mass of humanity.

With the flood of individuals from the countryside added to an already crowded city, the basic first question was, "Where are they going to live?"

Many of them simply found a tiny vacant piece of land and occupied it, or more accurately, squatted upon it. If a person settled on a piece of land, and his ownership was not challenged—it was his. Complete and total confusion best describes the ownership of land in Saigon.

These recent arrivals were truly squatters. Again, there was no way that these people could be counted. However, estimates pronounced that ten percent of the people in the city fell into this category.

Just exactly what was a squatter? Well, he was a newcomer to Saigon who arrived after 1960. The average family numbered five to six children. The father was an unskilled laborer whose pay was low, perhaps much less than one hundred dollars per month. If they were old enough, some of his children also worked.

His house was built from scraps, salvage material, anything that he could get his hands on. This included cardboard, plywood, canvas, and, hopefully, salvage metal, if he could find it. He tried to install wooden floors, but these very soon would begin to rot. Although some squatters had money, the majority were poverty-stricken. Desperate to find living space, many had to resort to taking up residence over a canal. Because of totally inadequate sewage disposal throughout the city, the canals became glorified septic tanks. When the tide was up, there was no smell, but when the tide was down the stench could be awful.

A small handful of city residents, perhaps five percent at most, were wealthy families who resided in old French villas, or occupied fine, new homes that were built in recent years. Many, many others lived in one- or two-story homes that were built of concrete blocks or mortar, and were covered with metal roofs.

At least thirty percent of the people were forced to live not too much differently than the squatters, in filthy crowded slums. What I would find remarkable was that girls wearing *ao dais* whose pants were white would somehow walk out of their dirty homes in the slums in fresh, neat, absolutely spotless attire. To me, a most impressive achievement.

Saigon was further handicapped by the fickle finger of fate. In this case blame could be placed on geography or environment. Of the city's eleven districts, four of them occupied land that was lower than in the rest of the city. Consequently, these areas became swamped during the rainy season each year. Small wonder that these four districts were the least densely populated. Increasing the population of those districts would have required extensive land development, for which the funds required were totally out of reach.

Other large cities have found solutions to crowding by building upward, thus taking maximum advantage of the space available. A prime example is Kowloon in Hong Kong. Kowloon has built high, wide, huge apartment buildings with each structure divided into so many tiny, tight apartments that the buildings resemble rabbit warrens.

But such was not a solution for Saigon. The city rests on soft clay soils. Buildings, consequently, were erected with wood and brick, and, as has been mentioned, most were low—limited to one or two stories.

High-rise apartments in Saigon would require steel reinforcing. Here, again, to erect enough structures to significantly improve the crowding problem was far beyond the city's and the nation's financial capabilities.

Some wag declared that the city was nothing but a sardine can stuffed with people. Alarmingly, with so much crowding, public health was the dominant concern. Exacerbating the public health problem were the mountains of garbage that could be found in all parts of the city. This was one problem that was being aggressively and successfully tackled. Nevertheless, as someone pointed out, many parts of Saigon still smelled like rotting fruit. It was perfectly obvious that radical sanitation measures were required in such a crowded city since disease, as it had before, could spread through the city like a wildfire.

The very basic municipal services that Americans expect and take for granted in their cities and towns, large and small, were major problems and challenges to the city of Saigon. A few are highlighted below:

Water: Saigon had been supplied water by twenty-seven wells. Very recently, a water treatment plant was opened and began pumping water into the city. Yet, even with this new development, over half of the city still obtained its water from wells. And the new purified water was being delivered through the city's old, often rusted, cast iron pipes. So even those receiving purified water had to guarantee its purity by boiling it before drinking it.

Sewage: The old sewage system left by the French had become totally and completely inadequate. Many people used the septic tanks that the city was able to pump out. But, appallingly, a frightening amount of raw sewage was being discharged into open bodies of water all over the city. This was an invitation to disaster.

Electricity: Five of the eleven districts that were situated on the edges of the city had no electricity. Power was sporadic, even in the good districts.

Roads: In the mid-sixties Saigon was subjected to a large-scale motorcycle invasion. On top of that, the number of taxis radically multiplied. There were at least seven thousand licensed taxis, with an uncounted number not licensed. The number of vehicles was at least five times greater than it had been fifteen years before. Undoubtedly, the constant pounding by the voluminous traffic forced yet another major problem—that of maintaining old streets and building new ones. An obvious concurrent problem was traffic safety. With so many individuals wanting to "get there fast," and becoming impatient and frustrated by constant slow moving traffic and bottlenecks, there were bound to be accidents. And there were many of them and, unfortunately, all too often, there were fatalities.

Talk about urban ills. Saigon had every single problem faced by major cities around the world. And because of Saigon's unique and peculiar situation, those problems were magnified.

But that is not all. Saigon's difficulties and complexities continued to abound. It possessed a situation shared by no other major city anywhere in the world. Saigon was the capital city of a country at war. There were constant violent reminders. There was no immediate danger of hordes of North Vietnamese soldiers invading from the North. However, there was constant evidence that members of the Viet Cong lived and worked in Saigon, and they were the immediate enemy. They were the terrorists. They were the ones who would place a bomb in a billeting or dining area; who would lob a hand grenade at a place where people gathered; who would fire rifles haphazardly from small, speeding cars or motorcycles. It was the fourteen-year-old son of a Viet Cong father who would attach a grenade to the accelerator pedal of an American jeep. When the American soldier started his jeep, it would blow up around him.

And far more frightening and distressing were the 120mm rockets. These would hit without any warning, reminiscent of the buzz bomb attacks on London during World War II. The rocket shots were haphazard, unaimed, hit-and-run. They caused extensive destruction. Not only would one greatly damage any structure that it hit, but also it would leave behind an enormous crater. These were always viewed by throngs of people. The damage and the crater had a demoralizing effect. The arrival of a 120mm rocket and its aftereffects would quickly be known throughout the city. This certainly was not good for morale.

A truism—one could never rest easy in Saigon.

This is the city in which I began my residence in September of 1967. This is the city that I would soon know intimately, and many of whose problems would become my problems.

SETTING THE STAGE

CHAPTER 3
WHAT WAS HAC?

What exactly was that command called HAC that we are talking about?

The United States Army Headquarters Area Command (USA-HAC, HAC) was established on April 1, 1966. It was a unique command, organized for a unique purpose, with a unique mission in an absolutely distinctive capital city of a country at war. What made this command so different and so unusual was that it was the only one in the American army. Even more significantly, it was the only one the army ever had, and they would never again have another like it.

It had to be special, for the situation for which it was created was very special, and that special situation was a city called Saigon.

For Saigon there was no parallel. It was a teeming metropolis of approximately three million people. The city was wide open, with perpetually jammed streets and a most heterogeneous population. The "Pearl of the Orient" was a fascinating but very complex community. It had every problem and challenge of a huge crowded city, and many more that were distinct unto itself. For example, there was hardly a spot on earth that provided a greater challenge to law and order. Police work was demanding, sensitive, complex and dangerous. It included problems of unprecedented difficulty and magnitude.

To complicate matters almost to an extreme—Saigon was in a combat zone. Within its confines there lived and worked many members of the devious, treacherous, murderous Viet Cong. They mixed with and were a part of the general populace. They were smiling, extremely friendly, good citizens. They could be the barber who cheerfully cut your hair during the day and tried to cut your throat at night. Their surreptitious activities resulted not only in casualties, but damage, and caused constant fear and unrest.

Tangible evidence that there was a war on and that Saigon was a big target came periodically, and when least expected. Huge rockets landed randomly and exploded.

Within the metropolitan area among the teeming Saigon millions, there lived and worked American military personnel, Department of Defense civilians, members of the diplomatic corps, TV personnel, newspaper reporters and journalists. Also stationed in the area, and for which the U.S. had responsibilities, were Free World Military Assistance forces from Korea, Thailand, Australia, New Zealand, and the Philippines. All of these together numbered in excess of thirty-five thousand individuals. Additionally, there were constantly on-leave or passing-through American military personnel, as well as diplomats and members of the media. This constant influx greatly swelled the number of "foreigners" who had plopped themselves down amongst the already overcrowded citizenry, who were desperately and mightily striving and straining just to survive.

It is perfectly obvious that these intruding Americans of every shade and stripe, together with their allies, were challenged by this strange, complex, and often chaotic environment. Thus, it was manifestly clear that they would require in their everyday living tremendous assistance and support.

And here is where HAC stepped in.

That command was created to meet that critical need. It came into being to provide administrative and logistical support, as well as law and order and security to those individuals brought into Saigon by the deep and extensive American commitment in Vietnam.

So HAC's primary and fundamental purpose for existing was to support, assist, and serve the people, so that they could fulfill whatever role they had in that city. HAC endeavored to make life as pleasant and safe as possible for them.

Virtually every individual would be touched in some way by HAC in different ways, and some in many ways—all of them—the military, diplomats, journalists, government workers, private citizens, as well as the members of the Free World Military Assistance forces. Yet, there is a great irony here. Many would take for granted the services and support that they received, and most would never know who it was that provided them.

I, as Commanding General, USAHAC, was assigned to and under the command of the Commanding General, United States Army, Vietnam (CG, USARV), and I operated under his direct supervision.

The Commanding General of USARV directed that I would fulfill administrative responsibilities and provide administrative support within the Saigon area for U.S. Army forces and other U.S. and Free World Military Assistance forces, as directed by his headquarters. The Saigon area was considered to be those urban and suburban areas known as Saigon, Cholon, and Tan Son Nhut, less Tan Son Nhut Air Base.

He specified that all USARV units within the administrative boundaries of USAHAC Saigon would comply with my directives, regardless of the owning command.

We have all heard that ol' cliché about going from A to Z. Well, CG USARV assigned to me what he called "specific functions." These did not go from A to Z, but astonishingly they *did* go all the way from A to Y. When one reads this extensive, exhaustive, all-encompassing list, he must conclude that surely CG USARV could have come up with one more specific function to round it out to A to Z.

When reading these widely divergent functions and responsibilities, one must also conclude that when those in authority had tasks to assign, and could not decide where to place them, HAC was the handy, available, convenient place to drop them—so they did.

The vast array of specific functions was the widest and broadest, and the responsibilities were the most extensive, all encompassing that I had ever encountered during my long years of military service. And they were *mine*—all mine. They rested squarely in my lap.

Initially there was some consternation, for I had some difficulty comprehending all that I was supposed to do. Even now, many years later, I find it difficult to describe all that CG USARV tasked me to do. But they say that seeing is believing, so what better way for the reader to understand my challenge than to read it from A to Y exactly as it was presented to me. So, here it goes.

Specific Functions and Responsibilities of USAHAC, Saigon for the Saigon Installation Area.

a. Base Development Planning.

b. Liaison with civilian authorities.

c. Maintain law and order, suppress and investigate crime. Insure that uniform regulations are enforced and that a high standard of military courtesy is observed. Operate Military Police and courtesy patrols. Provide police services for the greater Saigon/Cholon/Tan Son Nhut area. In addition provide joint motor patrols with the Vietnamese National Police on the Bien Hoa Highway Route IA.

d. Physical security of installations to include access control, interior guard, security fencing and lighting, and security discipline.

e. Morale, welfare and recreation, to include Special Service activities.

f. Publication and administration of a safety program.

g. Publication and enforcement of pass, leave, and liberty regulations.

h. Operation of all clubs and messes except for field ration messes of TOE units, and those open messes presently under the control of Hq. USARV.

i. Operation of all permanent and transient billeting except troop billeting under the control of Hq. USARV.

j. Operation of all administrative motor pools, except those operated by TOE units or TD units assigned to the command of TOE units.

k. Area Damage Control.

l. Provide, administer, and coordinate denominational and area religious coverage.

m. Provide required transportation services.

n. Coordinate the acquisition, allocation, and control of real estate.

o. Provide for repairs and utilities, insect and rodent control, sanitation, fire prevention, and fire protection services.

p. Operation of commissary stores and clothing sales stores, and provide household goods and baggage services.

q. Provide and administer financial services to include budgeting for the assigned area of responsibility, and country-wide accounting, disbursing, and funding as directed.

r. Plan and conduct inspections of assigned personnel, materiel, equipment and facilities, and of attached units as directed, to determine and evaluate organizational capabilities.

s. Coordinate the disposal of deceased personnel.

t. Provide in-service educational and counseling service in the area of responsibility, to include maintenance of records, conduct of end of course examinations and tests for USAFI courses, to include the establishment of a testing section for the administration of GED tests.

u. Provide the administration of University of Maryland Overseas Program for all the Republic of Vietnam.

v. Acquire, terminate, allocate, control, and manage real estate within Tan Son Nhut Airbase, to include USOM area, which has been designated for U.S. Army use, to include U.S. Army units under operational control of MACV or any other headquarters. Direct coordination with units or headquarters concerned is authorized.

w. Functions as USARV representative on VNAF-USAF-USA-TSN Base Planning Board.

x. Provide administrative and logistical support to ACTIV to include billets, office and supply space, transportation, office equipment and supplies.

y. Coordinate for approval all U.S. military civic action projects in the Saigon/Cholon area, with the mayor of Saigon or appropriate Vietnamese governmental agencies, provide liaison and coordination with USAID, OCO and the voluntary charitable organization which support military civic action. Act as point of contact for U.S. military undertaking civic action projects in the area, and maintain a file of potential military civic action projects that will have the greatest impact upon the population of the Saigon/Cholon metropolitan area. Serve as advisor to the mayor of Saigon on U.S. military civic action matters.

Anyway you cut it, A to Y is a huge, huge mouthful. In fact, it was an extraordinarily overflowing plateful. It is small wonder that I was often jocularly referred to as the "*military* mayor" of Saigon.

Thus far about my responsibilities we have heard words, words, words. It is time to get specific, to put words into action. Just what is meant when we mention administrative and logistical support in Saigon, and law and order and security? *M* above simply states, "Provide required transportation services." This is a very simple phrase, an innocent sounding directive. But what exactly does it involve, entail? Just exactly—specifically—what did HAC do on behalf of all those individuals that it was directed to support?

Here are those specifics.

HAC:

1. **Fed people.** We operated all the messes and all the clubs. We served thirty thousand meals a day in twenty-two different messes. We also operated the only commissary in a combat theater since the Civil War. This commissary was a huge operation, and did hundreds of thousands of dollars worth of business each month.

2. **Housed people.** We were, then, one of the world's largest innkeepers. We provided billets for eleven thousand persons. We operated seventy-eight hotels of all sizes and capacities—all under my control. In addition to billets, we provided units with headquarters buildings, warehouses, motor pools, and other needs. When a unit or an individual needed a facility, he came to us. We located what was suitable, negotiated with the owner, signed the lease and paid the rent. We were responsible for 450 leased facilities, for which we paid a rent of twenty million dollars annually.

3. **Maintained people.** We provided repair, utilities, and minor construction for the 450 leased facilities that we occupied. These buildings were far below U.S. standards as to electrical circuitry, power, water. To compound the difficulty, they had not been built to house Americans, who took one or two showers daily, and who had air conditioners, stereos, hot plates. Maintenance was a constant and challenging problem.

4. **Transported people.** We operated the largest non-tactical motor pool in the U.S. Army. Our fleet consisted of over two thousand vehicles, including sixty different makes and models. We operated a bus line with over 160 busses, and provided the necessary cars, jeeps, and trucks to move this extensive population and tons of supplies. We transported monthly over eight hundred thousand passengers, and covered with our vehicles over nine hundred thousand miles a month in crowded, teeming Saigon/Cholon. It was our responsibility to maintain, and to do the necessary repair work to keep running this aging, overworked fleet of two thousand vehicles.

5. **Provided law and order and secured people.** Undoubtedly our most important function. We were responsible for the security of all our people and all of our installations. The multitude of widely scattered installations and vast number of people greatly magnified the challenge. Security was provided by Military Police guards, and with Military Police day and night motorized patrols. In addition, each hotel and installation had a defense plan, and had been issued arms and ammunition for the defense of those installations. In addition to security, the military police were responsible for the law and order of the vast and varied number of people under our jurisdiction.

6. **Provided power.** We had operating 480 generators, from 10kw to 600kw, which provided necessary power for headquarters, communications, and many other miscellaneous facilities. The generators were constantly going full blast, and had to be constantly maintained and serviced to meet the demands placed upon them.

7. **Cooled people.** We were responsible for the installation and maintenance of over six thousand air conditioners.

8. **Watered people.** We provided water. All individuals needed potable water—the Saigon city supply was not potable. Therefore, it was our responsibility to produce potable water. We did this with twenty-one water purification plants of all sizes. After the potable water was produced, it had to be delivered. We had a fleet of water tankers constantly delivering potable water on an extremely tight schedule. Many installations needed non-potable water as well, and this was delivered as required.

9. **Clothed people.** By operating a clothing store, we certainly clothed people. The store did a monthly business of thirty-five thousand dollars.

10. **Operated recreational facilities.** Those facilities included indoor and outdoor theaters, a bowling alley, swimming pools, craft shops, library, boat club, gymnasium, basketball courts, and tennis courts.

11. **Provided church services.** On a given Sunday, we conducted thirty services at nineteen different locations.

From whatever perspective it is viewed, the list of tasks just outlined above that HAC performed in support of people is not only impressive, but also absolutely staggering. To properly appreciate the magnitude of the operation and achievement, one must recognize that we are talking about upwards of thirty-five thousand people collected together. We must certainly be aware that this number of people represents a good-sized city in America. So we are really describing a city within a city. But no city of thirty-five thousand in America could have a populace more widely scattered, less cohesive, with more varied and diverse reasons for being than the elements that HAC was tasked to support. Without question, this was a most daunting challenge.

With all this in mind the time has now come to ask some inevitable and intriguing questions. How was HAC able to accomplish all the tasks required of it? Just what did it take to get the job done? It is appropriate at this point to paraphrase the wag who stated, "The difficult we can do right now—but the impossible takes a little longer." In many respects it was HAC that did the almost impossible.

It was absolutely astonishing that the magnitude of tasks could be balanced by such unbelievably limited resources. It is appropriate now to ask, "What were those limited resources?"

On the 31st of January 1968, the headquarters and headquarters detachment of USAHAC numbered seventy-one officers, seventeen warrant officers, and 628 enlisted personnel, for a total strength of 716. Yes, that figure is not a misprint, 716 Americans. Amazingly, 716 is less than the strength of the average American Army battalion.

Now the word "impossible" begins to have merit. We at HAC kept the situation from becoming impossible by taking to heart one of CG USARV's special instructions, which stated, "Local hire of personnel and contracting will be used in lieu of U.S. Army personnel where necessary to make up personnel shortfalls consistent with military security and mission requirements."

To get the job done we hired Vietnamese personnel. Working for HAC by January 31, 1968 were approximately 6,500 Vietnamese civilians. These individuals drove busses and trucks, maintained and repaired vehicles, cooked and served in messes, serviced air conditioners and generators, operated water points, did repair and small construction work on facilities, did housekeeping in the billets, and many were even used as civilian security guards.

But it was HAC personnel who screened, hired, trained, assigned, and continually coordinated and supervised this small army of workers. The Vietnamese employed by HAC, fortunately, were quick learners, conscientious, dedicated, hardworking, loyal, responsive, and completely dependable. Without them the mission could never have been accomplished—it would have been mission impossible. Many of them moved into leadership positions, and aided, immeasurably, the limited number of HAC personnel. These key Vietnamese members of HAC were delegated responsibilities for screening, selecting, and training Vietnamese workers, and coordinated and supervised their efforts.

But, as stated before, the most critical and demanding mission assigned to HAC by far was the law and order and security mission. As part of its overall security mission, HAC was charged with the responsibility of adequate physical security of installations under its control. This included the provision of guard personnel, protecting from hostile actions those facilities for which the occupants had no reasonable capability to provide guards for themselves, and for the maintenance of a priority list of installations and activities to be guarded in accordance with the availability of military and guard personnel.

Broadly speaking, HAC was geared to and prepared for terrorist attacks that might occur at any time in the city. The form of those terrorist attacks could be a bomb in a hotel billet or dining area, a hand grenade thrown at a bus or where people gathered, such as in the commissary or at church services, or haphazard sniper fire and small arms attacks. Such activity had occurred in the past. With the increase in strength and aggressiveness of the Viet Cong, that type of activity was bound to occur at any time, and would surely increase in frequency. HAC, of course, was responsible for being prepared to cope with and react to such activity.

The criticality of the security mission logically prompts the question, "Well, just what tools, what resources, did HAC possess that enabled it to accomplish this important and often dangerous mission?"

During the early months of 1967, as tension increased throughout Vietnam, there was, likewise, a perceptible increase in tension in Saigon. In order to meet the greatly expanding security requirements, it was agreed that HAC needed augmentation. Accordingly, 242 enlisted men were placed on duty with USAHAC during mid 1967 for 180 days of temporary duty. These men received ten days of training, and then were assigned posts as security guards. None of these individuals had received any combat advanced individual training (AIT), nor had any unit been provided with tactical training. In this respect they were similar in background to the other personnel assigned to HAC.

By December 1967 the requirement for these additional security guards not only persisted but also crystallized. So on January 1, 1968 they were assigned to USAHAC, and organized into the Security Guard Company (Provisional). Additionally, the 34th Finance Section (Funding) was attached to HAC. The strength of the Security Guard Company (Provisional) was two Officers and 194 Enlisted Men. These additional elements brought the strength of USAHAC from 716 to 931. However, in the case of the Security Guard Company, this latest addition was added for a special, specific, and narrow purpose—that of security—and would have no impact whatsoever upon the execution of the other broad HAC missions.

As stated before, of all the missions assigned to HAC, the law and order and security one was, without question, preeminent. It was considered so important, so critical that, since HAC did not have the necessary resources, it was provided with yet another assist, a tremendously important one. HAC was given a tool that was powerful, appropriate, and perfectly and expertly honed for the task. That tool was the 716th Military Police Battalion. That unit, reputedly, at that time was the largest military police battalion in the U.S. Army with a strength of approximately 1,100.

The 716th had been placed under my *operational* command. This may not have been the first time, but it undoubtedly was one of the very rare times that a military police unit of this size and organization was placed under a *non*-MPs operational command. This was a development that the military police hierarchy had great difficulty accepting. More than that, it raised their hackles, and was to them a constant irritant. They were more than aware that Saigon provided every challenge and test—and then some—that a Military Policeman and a Military Police unit could ever be called upon to face. Especially unsettling to the Military Police Corps was the very high visibility that the MPs had in Saigon. Their vehicles, uniforms, and especially their helmets and helmet liners were distinctive, and their presence was constantly noted and felt, as they were everywhere—covering the Saigon metropolitan area like a blanket. Yet, their operational directives, instructions, and orders came from me—the non MP.

Yes, for some, very difficult to accept.

Within the HAC organization, we had a small security, plans, and operations directorate. This staff element broke down my broad law and order and security missions into specific operations, tasks, and assignments—the "nuts and bolts." These were further developed with the cooperation and coordination of the key members of the 716th MP Battalion. It was only after all this that they were ordered to be implemented.

As a commander, I was not about to assign a mission or task to a type unit that I had not previously commanded, without ensuring that it had the resources and the capability to carry them out.

In addition to the 716th I had placed under my operational command the 90th Military Police Detachment. This unit was specifically assigned to me, so that I would have a Provost Marshal capability. The commander of this detachment would be a valued member of my staff, and would be my direct agent located in downtown Saigon. His office would conduct itself like the main desk at police headquarters in a large American city.

So for security purposes I had under my direct operational command the MP Battalion and the Provost Marshal. Another development, as I have mentioned, was the inclusion within USAHAC of the Security Guard Company. This was a force of nearly two hundred men. Although this unit was not nearly as well trained or as capable as the military police, their total reason in being involved security.

The last thing I wanted was to have two separate units under my command tackling identical security missions. I knew that this could well result in awkward situations, and could involve competition, over lapping, "dropping of the ball" recriminations, finger pointing. It was necessary to ensure that there be unity of effort and a completely professional approach to the difficult and diverse security missions. Accordingly, I attached the Security Guard Company to the 716th MP Battalion. This increased the strength of the battalion to approximately 1300. The Security Guard Company would never appear to be another MP company. It took only one glance to recognize the difference. Its uniform was that of a conventional army unit, and did not have the color and distinctive flair of an MP.

And here was a great irony. HAC's right arm, the MP Battalion, a subordinate element, was, with its attachments, in considerably greater strength than all the rest of HAC. Another irony: there was not an individual in Saigon, foreign or domestic, who was not aware on a daily basis of the presence of the MPs. Yet virtually no one in the city was aware that the MPs operated under a headquarters and that the headquarters was USAHAC. Most assumed, if they thought about it at all, that the MPs were an entity, that they were out there operating independently.

Another connection not understood was HAC and the Provost Marshal. With him as a member of my staff, and his detachment under my operational command, I chose to delegate to him significant and extensive responsibilities. After all, he was my police expert. So he had the authority to handle directly law and order matters.

As Provost Marshal, he was my agent in downtown Saigon. In cities around America, police problems went directly to the police desk. In Saigon, police problems went directly to the Provost Marshal. He received the calls. He would make a quick analysis of the problem, and decide on what measures were required to solve or eliminate it. In most cases the immediate deployment of MPs was necessary. The Provost Marshal did not dispatch the MPs himself. He would levy the requirement on the 716th, who always had elements in readiness, and who would immediately send out the necessary force.

Because the Provost Marshal and the Commanding Officer of the 716th were Military Police "pros," a familiar and easy working routine developed. I had great confidence in both of them, and without hesitation delegated great authority to them. My staff and I stayed out of the way, and let them run the Military Police "show."

I was in constant contact with both, and was kept aware of the type problems that were cropping up, patterns that might be developing, difficulties that could be anticipated. Thus, I always had an up to date assessment of the law and order and security *climate* in Saigon.

As was inevitable, there were occasions when the Provost Marshal asked the 716th for forces they considered unnecessary, excessive, or inappropriate to solve or eliminate a problem. If the dispute could not be readily settled, and if there was no emergency, the matter was brought to my headquarters where members of my staff, or I, resolved it. In an emergency the call came directly to me, and I made my decision on the spot.

I was completely confident that the necessary command and control was in place, and that our SOP (standard operating procedure) for law and order and security was professional and effective.

Basically it was a very harmonious operation.

With the big pile that HAC and I already had sitting in our laps we never expected, and certainly did not need, the "high, fast pitch" that was thrown at us on September 18, 1967.

On that date United States Army Headquarters Area Command was placed under the *operational control* of Commander, United States Military Assistance Command, Vietnam (COMUSMACV)—General William Westmoreland. Command, *less* operational control, was vested in Commanding General, United States Army, Vietnam (CGUSARV)—Lieutenant General Bruce Palmer.

The Bible tells us that we cannot serve two masters. Well, there I was being called upon to do just that—to serve the two most powerful, demanding military masters in Vietnam. That development did nothing to simplify our operation. Rather, it posed more and greater challenges. It was very important to remember those command distinctions when totally unexpected events subsequently occurred.

I have described in extreme and, perhaps, exhaustive detail just who and what HAC was. I believe that it was necessary to do this because one must have a clear picture of what HAC was in order to be able to understand and appreciate just what it was *not*.

HAC was not a tactical headquarters. None of its enlisted personnel were tactical soldiers. They did *not* come from the combat arms, infantry, armor, artillery. None had received advanced infantry training (AIT), nor had they trained or maneuvered as part of a tactical unit.

HAC's headquarters had no responsibility for or capability of intelligence gathering, and no communications network. It was by means of coordination with various agencies and headquarters that USAHAC obtained intelligence and information on the tactical situation in the area.

The 716th Military Police Battalion, likewise, was *not* a combat arms battalion. The members of this unit habitually carried, had often fired, and were very familiar with various types of small arms. Most had been exposed to some infantry training. Theirs was demanding physical work. They were constantly being confronted with troubling situations that often put them at risk and in considerable danger. Wherever they operated, they were armed. But they were trained primarily as policemen—to do police work. They were specialists and had received extensive training in their specialty. They had a high degree of expertise—were an extremely well trained, efficient, capable military police unit. But their training had not been geared to, or qualified them fully for infantry battalion missions.

So there it is—a very detailed discussion of what USAHAC was. And a quick, brief glimpse at what it was *not.*

This distinction will be of great importance when analyzing and assessing the totally unexpected role into which would soon be thrust.

SETTING THE STAGE

CHAPTER 4
PRELUDE TO COUNTRYWIDE ATTACK AT TET

During the early hours of Wednesday, January 31, 1968 tens of thousands of guerrillas materialized out of the darkness in South Vietnam and hit communities of every size and description throughout the country. These forces hit fifty hamlets, sixty-four district capitals, thirty-six provincial capitals, which were major South Vietnamese population centers, and five autonomous cities throughout South Vietnam. This widespread offensive brought war to the cities for the first time.

The attack was totally unexpected and a complete surprise. It was a shot heard 'round the world. Its magnitude was shocking, staggering. Even more unbelievable was that it had "kicked off" on the most precious, sacred Vietnamese holiday, TET, the Lunar New Year.

This absolutely audacious offensive in South Vietnam, in a single stroke, dramatically and unquestionably altered the complexion of the Vietnam War. It would turn out to be the watershed event of that war. That was the day that the war was lost in the hearts and minds of most Americans. They just could not reconcile the optimistic "light at the end of the tunnel" rhetoric of our leaders with the TV footage of U.S. troops engaged in a full blown fight with the Viet Cong sappers in the U.S. Embassy Compound in downtown Saigon.

How did this happen? Where did it come from? What was its genesis? What did they hope to achieve?

For many months the war, for the Communists, had been going extremely well. The tactics of their forces on the battlefield had been extremely successful. They were controlling the battlefield. They avoided battle except on the ground of their choosing. Importantly, they were the ones who established those most critical elements in combat—time and place.

Their battlefield strategy was sound, and their operations were well planned and carefully designed. Theirs were attacks by small- to medium-sized units that were executed accurately and aggressively. They cleverly drew U.S. personnel into prepared "killing zones." Theirs were surgical strikes. The almost daily small-scale actions were progressively increasing the number of American casualties. But more importantly, the frustration at not being able to box in this slippery, elusive opponent was succeeding in raising the American fighting man's anxiety level, and was taking large bites out of his self confidence.

These attacks were limited attacks on carefully selected terrain. They were absolute masters of their own environment, while the Americans found it strange, completely foreign and especially intimidating. This placed the Americans at a great disadvantage, and ensured for the Vietnamese a great tactical advantage.

These continuing attacks kept the American forces off balance, on the defensive, and constantly *reacting*. This absolutely unconventional war, in all its aspects, kept the Americans rocking back on their heels.

But as time passed, the resourceful American fighting man began to adjust to the terrain and to the enemy tactics. Additionally, the number of their forces that were engaged increased in strength. The Americans continued to react, but now more aggressively and effectively.

This began to have a telling effect on the enemy. The Communist ground tactics became progressively less effective, the tide began to turn, and the changing nature of events brought a sense of discouragement new to the enemy ground forces. Leaders began to be alarmed at the devastating losses that U.S. firepower was gradually inflicting on the Communist ranks in the South.

The Communist leaders were faced with a new and increasingly severe problem—heavy and telling strikes from the air.

There was a sense of impotency beginning to develop as American planes continued to pound away at North Vietnamese transportation and communications centers, curtailing the flow of food and consumer goods throughout the country, as well as military material in from China.

They tried to cope with what they ultimately recognized as, in the long run, a strategically hopeless situation. Firepower was eating deeper and deeper into their reserves of men and arms. The leaders were now reconciled to the startling realization and belief that the Viet Cong and North Vietnamese forces could not hold out many months longer against the U.S. and its allies.

One Hanoi official had become so pessimistic that he declared, "If we keep fighting this way for five more years, all that will be left of Vietnam will be a desert."

So, as far back as the spring of 1967 earnest discussions began taking place.

The leaders began to seriously re-examine their long-standing strategy of waging a protracted war of attrition from rural base areas. This just did not seem to be working any longer. It was time to end the war of attrition—the drawn-out guerrilla war.

Of utmost and immediate importance was slowing or reversing the gradually increasing momentum of the American effort. Of vital concern was the need to somehow deescalate the war before it got too big for them to handle. A dramatic turnaround was desperately needed. It was obvious to them that to accomplish this something different had to be done, that a radical change in strategy was required. They had to decide on something very big, something monumental, something that would change the whole course of the war, that would enable them to achieve victory in the shortest possible time.

Recognizing that this was a daunting challenge, the Communist high command met with great purpose in Hanoi in July of 1967. This group included political and military leaders from the North as well as high-level Communist sympathizers from South Vietnam. In addition, North Vietnam recalled its foreign ambassadors to attend this meeting. Thus, this turned out to be as powerful a group as the Communist hierarchy could gather together.

Within the ranks of the high command that met in Hanoi, there were five who were considered the most powerful and influential. There were the big three: General Giap, Ho Chi Minh, and Pham Van Dong. The fourth leading figure was Le Duan who supported the big three, but with some reservations, and the fifth was Truong Chinh, whose role was unclear.

During a crisis, even amongst a powerful group, there invariably is an individual who emerges as the leader, the "take charge guy," the one who rises to the occasion, the one whose shoulders the others load with responsibilities, the one who will make the crucial and necessary decisions.

Such an individual was North Vietnamese Defense Minister, General Vo Nguyen Giap. General Giap was already a very well known quantity. He had already been severely tested, and more than met those challenges. He was a master tactician, the great victor of the Viet Minh War against the French, and thus far the supreme strategist of the war against the U.S. General Giap was one of the best tactical commanders of the twentieth century.

He was by nature a cautious man who preferred to act after all the loose ends were tied. In this situation, however, he knew that he was working against time, trying to cope with a situation that was increasingly becoming more difficult. He well knew that his associates had become alarmed at being forced into a defensive posture. They wanted to change that with little delay, so General Giap was feeling the pressure.

The group had decided that the time was ripe for a crowning psychological event. They were ready, if necessary, to take a huge gamble, to carry out one decisive, massive battle, to grab onto anything, regardless of how bold, to knock the American effort back on its heels. Certainly, a drastic, dramatic move was required to deescalate the war.

So General Giap made a startling proposal that resulted in a portentous decision by this collection of top leaders. Thus, about mid July the concept of the TET offensive was born.

General Giap had proposed a general offensive, a surprise nation wide offensive. He believed that such an offensive would have a huge secondary effort, that it would trigger a popular and general uprising. So Hanoi named it the General Offensive/General Uprising. General Giap and all the others firmly believed that once the offensive was underway that the civilians in the South would rally firmly to their cause.

To greatly multiply the chances of success for this bold, daring operation, he made another earth shaking proposal. He urged the leaders to agree that the offensive coincide with the TET holidays, that it take place during the next Lunar New Year festival. This, of course, was blasphemous.

Yes, he well recognized the sacrilege of waging war during TET. He knew that this would not only offend many Vietnamese, but would cause great shock and dismay to his countrymen. However, he was convinced that he was assured of a total and complete surprise, as the festival would provide the perfect cover for his operation.

To salve his conscience, somewhat, he certainly must have looked back to 1789 for an historic precedent. During that year, Vietnamese patriots had attacked Chinese in Hanoi during the Lunar New Year festival. That is the only known case of military activity at TET. However, he must have conveniently overlooked one big difference. This time the enemy was attacking not only Americans, but their own countrymen as well. It was a case of Vietnamese fighting Vietnamese on the most sacred of holidays.

Supplies had for some time been proceeding at a slow, tortuous pace. So by scheduling the launching of his offensive during the Lunar New Year, he hoped that it would provide him with the lead-time he required.

He decided that he would use Southern Viet Cong soldiers rather than Northern troops, where possible.

Giap would radically depart from the tactics and strategy that they had utilized up until now. They would abandon tactical efforts in the countryside, and for the very first time, they would carry the fighting only into the urban centers, which had been previously untouched.

The offensive would concentrate on airfields, air support activities, military headquarters, civilian governmental complexes, materiel and logistic centers, as well as the thirty-six largest cities and towns in the country.

His goals and objectives were definitely lofty and ambitious. He hoped that he would force the Americans to crack militarily and psychologically; that aircraft, communications, transportation, and the well-coordinated command centers—which he regarded as the real American strength—would be destroyed. Further, he envisioned that the South Vietnamese Army would disintegrate, and the populace would rise up in massive support of the Communists.

Preparations had moved along pretty much on schedule. So by mid January 1968 the exact time and date for the "kick off," the start of the offensive, was set.

Poised for the attack were 240,000 Communist troops, of which 65,000 were assigned to take part in the first-wave assault on the cities.

General Giap moved his headquarters to a command post in the southern panhandle of North Vietnam. He believed that he was about to strike a catastrophic blow at his enemies, who were American as well as South Vietnamese.

It was only General Giap, among all the North and South Vietnamese Communists, who could have organized and supervised the extremely elaborate synchronization of the TET offensive.

There were several important factors that played right into Giap's hands. Some he had anticipated; others fell into his lap.

Members of the South Vietnamese Army had been carrying out so called pacification efforts. Thus, on the eve of TET they were disbursed in a myriad of garrisons around the countryside.

On top of that—following a long standing tradition at TET—

half of the Army of the Republic of Vietnam (ARVN) would be on leave and with their families.

For several months before TET, U.S. policymakers—civilian and military alike—persisted in painting a rosy picture of the military situation in Vietnam. Many Americans, accordingly, were lulled into thinking that the war was well on the way to being won, and would be totally unprepared for the great shock of TET.

At the same time, Giap was well aware that not all Americans were "buying" the assessment that was being presented. Public demonstrations and protests were strong indications that dissension was growing, and that the war was not a popular one. American troops in Vietnam were well aware of the "goings on." It was hurtful to know that the folks back home were not fully supporting them in their most difficult of assignments, and so a bit of pessimism was creeping, as well, into the ranks of the troops in Vietnam.

A conference attended by high level American military and civilian leaders met in Hawaii during the summer of 1967. The U.S. was heavily involved and deeply embroiled in a war in Vietnam. It was time, they well knew, to develop a strategy for winning and thus ending that war. Amazingly, when the conference broke up, no strategy had been agreed upon. This was in sharp contrast to what occurred in Hanoi in July of 1967.

The first and most holy day of TET in 1968 was January 30. All-out celebrations began that night. Revelry knew no bounds. Impossible to comprehend was that while the firecrackers were snapping, popping, and bouncing, there lurked in the woodwork all over the country elements that in a matter of just a couple of hours would suddenly smother the celebrations with a nationwide "wet" blanket.

TET, from those early hours on Jan. 31,1968, was cast in a totally different light; it would never be the same. The word TET would henceforth and forever be associated with the TET of 1968—the TET offensive.

SETTING THE STAGE

CHAPTER 5
PRELUDE TO THE TET ATTACK ON SAIGON

When the Communists prepared for their attack across the length and breadth of South Vietnam, they saw out there a wide array of significant, vulnerable targets. But of them all, the city of Saigon was unquestionably the most mouthwatering. After all it was the major city, the capital city, the nerve center of the nation that was their enemy in their current war.

And in downtown Saigon, in the heart of the city, rested that new and most imposing structure—the United States Embassy. The Embassy was the most visible reminder of that hated intruder who was popping up everywhere, and fighting in support of their rival Vietnamese regime.

They were completely aware and it was absolutely clear to them that Saigon and the U.S. Embassy were unparalleled psychological targets. If they could capture the Embassy, and seize other pre designated targets like the Presidential Palace, governmental and military buildings and compounds, they would gain control of Saigon.

Word would quickly spread to every corner of the world that the capital city and the U.S. Embassy had been captured. Even more striking would be the realization that with the fall of its Embassy, the North American giant would not only be humbled but humiliated. Capturing the Embassy would be a strike at the heart of America. As a symbol, its capture would prove to the Vietnamese, the American people, and the rest of the world that the "imperialist power" was, indeed, vulnerable.

There is no question that the moment the decision was made to launch an attack upon Saigon, preparations for the seizure of that city began to take shape.

The Viet Cong were given five months training for the TET offensive, including street fighting in mock up villages in the jungle. They were told to fill water canteens with gasoline and to use them to burn houses that would provide them with an escape route in the confusion, if they were surrounded.

They had no plans in case of failure. They were told that if they had problems, they would be reinforced or relieved by other forces. Better yet, all firmly believed that the South Vietnamese elements would cross over to the attackers and join the fight against the Americans.

Plans included kidnapping youths as young as fourteen years of age from their homes in the villages outside Saigon just before the attack, giving them rifles, and ordering them to fight. Teenagers in Saigon were ready to join the fighting after they had been convinced by Viet Cong members that they were going to liberate the people from the American imperialists. Loyalties of families in Saigon were sharply mixed. Some were pleased and even enthusiastic about their alliance with and support of the Viet Cong, while many others scuttled hurriedly away as though they feared picking up a dreaded disease.

Many North Vietnamese were designated to be in support of the Viet Cong. They were primarily draftees who heard the familiar refrain from their authorities in North Vietnam that they would be welcomed as liberators.

Viet Cong elements had specific, pre designated targets. Just before the attack, these forces would move into town in groups of twos and threes and wait in private homes until they were ordered to attack. This infiltration would pose no problem, for they would have the perfect cover—the riotous celebrating and the fireworks.

Over a period of many weeks the leaders infiltrated into Saigon hundreds and perhaps even thousands of agents. These would blend into the landscape and would pose as normal Vietnamese going about their business.

Through a series of staging areas the North Vietnamese brought munitions over the border from Cambodia to the tunnels of Cu Chi and the "Iron Triangle." Selected men and women were assembled in the tunnels, where they received daily briefings. Systematically, people and weapons would be moved into the Saigon suburbs, and on the eve of the assault would be ready to gather in specially prepared safe houses inside Saigon.

The build up continued in many other ways. All during the fall, agents in the form of women and children moved in weapons, by a variety of subterfuges, past the city's checkpoints. The most numerous and commonplace of these was to conceal the weapons beneath agricultural produce in the wagons that were constantly entering Saigon in substantial numbers.

An extremely clever and most effective subterfuge was to hide weapons inside coffins as part of cleverly acted and arranged funeral processions. One of the busiest cemeteries was a military cemetery that closely adjoined Tan Son Nhut Air Base. There was hardly a day that passed without multiple funerals. If a witness had stood there making a daily count, he might have concluded that because of so many Saigon residents dying, there must be a plague at work somewhere in the city. Surprisingly, these all too frequent funerals and burials did not arouse any apparent suspicions. If there were individuals with suspicions, they certainly kept them to themselves.

Many NVA and Viet Cong officers took complete advantage of the available weeks before the assault to reconnoiter secretly their pre designated targets in Saigon. They moved freely around the city on forged identity papers. Fifth column soldiers and officers worked inside military installations.

In their planning, the NVA decided that among their targets to assault and capture they would include such lucrative installations as the ARVN armor and artillery schools. Once this was accomplished they would take over and operate the vehicles captured at the armor school, giving them much needed mobility and firepower. Similarly, an artillery team would man weapons captured from the artillery school, giving them a heavy weapons capability, which they lacked.

The Communists took advantage of the short Christmas truce for the final opportunity to reconnoiter a wide range of selected targets. The commander of the 9th Viet Cong Division, for example, personally inspected his unit's primary objective, Tan Son Nhut Air Base on the edge of Saigon, while his regimental commanders visited the "family gravesite" just outside the base.

One can only shake his head in wonder, and marvel at the tremendous and extremely rare military advantage that a commander acquires when he is able to see, examine, and actually "set foot on" the objective that he will soon be attacking. Here was such a case.

In Saigon the Mardi Gras atmosphere of the TET celebration would be at its peak when North Vietnamese Major General Tran Do entered his command post on the outskirts of the city. He was selected by the Central Office for South Vietnam (COSVN) to coordinate the offensive against Saigon. Tran Do, large for a Vietnamese, was a handsome, bull necked man of fifty. He would report directly by radio to a four star general and to Huynh Tan Phat, vice president of the National Liberation Front. In turn these two men, stationed at the main COSVN headquarters near the Cambodian border, would keep their superiors in North Vietnam informed on an hour to hour basis of the unfolding battle in Saigon.

Communist communications inside Saigon would be anything but sophisticated. Tran Do's commanders would have to rely on runners, often women and young boys. This system, naturally, lacked flexibility, and once the go signal would be given, there was little chance to reinforce one unit from another. As a result, highly motivated political cadres were charged with the duty of seeing to it that nothing went amiss. They were to march with their units and to die with them, if necessary.

Now a different look at this capital city just before it was rocked and shaken and turned upside down. Saigon, the capital city of a country at war, was a soft and sinful city. It was self-indulgent, and was not only ripe for, but invited the massive, unexpected blow that struck it during the early hours of 31 January 1968. It was caught—not napping—but sleeping. It was a relaxed city and mighty complacent as it sat over a ticking time bomb. For many of the residents of the city—both Vietnamese and American—the reality of the war out there somewhere in the "boondocks" did not seem to reach them. Yes, there was an occasional, isolated terrorist attack; sporadic small arms fire could sometimes be heard out there in the distance, and once in awhile a rare shell would be lobbed into the city from somewhere in the outskirts. Nothing to be concerned about—just part of the game.

The Vietnamese government, likewise, fled from reality. It apparently gave no serious thought to such expected wartime measures as rigid rationing, controls and compulsory savings. Instead of insisting on such stern measures, it compromised. This, of course, led to popular relaxation.

Before the TET attack, Saigon was presented as the capital of a small, poor, weak country in its ninth year of war for national survival. Yes, the country was short of everything important—teachers, schools, doctors, hospitals, clinics.

Yet, to celebrate the upcoming TET, hundreds, perhaps thousands of dollars a day were being spent for such extravagances as firecrackers.

It was traditional over the years to go on buying sprees in preparation for TET. This year conditions were not nearly the same. They cried out for restraint. But people nevertheless went ahead blindly with some reckless buying. There was much poverty in Saigon, but even here people purchased things that they could ill afford. Conversely, there was much prosperity with many "well heeled" individuals. These could afford and did go about purchasing gifts of the most luxurious nature. Those with American friends badgered them to pick up the choicest of items in the post exchange. Others picked out only the best, and paid triple the normal prices for legally imported luxury items such as Chanel No. 5 perfume, watches, cameras, TV sets, and the choicest brands of scotch and cognac.

In previous years the Vietnamese had begun to get "into the mood" about a month before the actual celebration. This year, as well, the holiday euphoria would last nearly a month. However, it appears that some concern should have been exhibited when the holiday truce proposals were whittled down to almost nothing. With the unprecedented "stirring around" that was taking place all over the country, there must have been wonder, rumors, even leaks. It is difficult to believe that the government was not being presented with some persistent warnings about an impending attack. If they had those warnings, they must have found them disbelieving and ignored them for they chose not to crack down on TET euphoria, and to order soldiers on TET leave to return to duty. Instead, the government lifted the important midnight to 4:00 A.M. curfew, which was a clear indication that the "guard was down," and was a virtual invitation to the enemy.

Softness permeated the Vietnamese regime, the civil service, the police, and the military. Vietnam had its percentage of honest men, and even individuals who endeavored to bring reform, but the whole atmosphere encouraged a spirit of "live and let live."

But the Americans in Saigon were every bit as relaxed and complacent as the Vietnamese.

Americans, largely because of HAC, lived the good life; they "had it made in the shade." They occupied comfortable hotel rooms of which there were many. The rooms had air conditioning and enough water for drinking and multiple showers. There were military messes in a variety of locations throughout the city that provided excellent chow to military personnel, and very reasonable rates for others who were eligible to use them. For those who wanted variety, there were an ample number of Vietnamese restaurants that served varied menus and delicious meals.

Many American civilians had access not only to the post exchange but to a commissary and clothing sales store, as well. They could attend a movie, bowl, play tennis, work in craft shops, draw books from a library—it was all there, all the comforts of home.

Many of Saigon's "Who's Who" of Americans gathered nightly

on the roof of the Rex Hotel, one of the larger billets under HAC's control. It was large and spacious, and could accommodate a sizeable crowd. There were bright hanging lights, and in three directions a magnificent view of metropolitan Saigon. But the centerpiece was the large and well-stocked bar, which was able to satisfy most thirsts and tastes.

Here, gathered nightly, were TV writers, cameramen, journalists, those serving in the Embassy, representatives of the various governmental agencies at work in Vietnam, the military—pundits of every stripe. Here the conversation was loud, never flagged, and the words often opinionated and plentiful. On most nights, one could quickly learn how the war in Vietnam could and should be won. Discussed, also, were many of the world's problems, which on the roof of the Rex could readily be solved.

If individuals wished to extend their evening after a few drinks, they could take the elevator from the roof to the street, and in a few moments could enjoy the company of beautiful, diminutive, trim, young ladies fetchingly attired in their split skirt *ao dais*.

That was Saigon on the eve of TET.

Crater remaining after an occasional, haphazard rocket explodes in Saigon.

HAC AT WAR

CHAPTER 6
TET CELEBRATION BEGINS

It was Tuesday, January 30, 1968 in Saigon, the capital city of South Vietnam. The day was bright and sunny—extremely pleasant—and the heat was far less oppressive than normal. In the headquarters building of the United States Army Headquarters Area Command all personnel seemed exceptionally bright, cheerful, light-hearted. All were well aware that the day was a unique, very special, exceptional one in Vietnam. The entire populace of the country on this day would begin to celebrate TET, the huge national holiday they had looked forward to, and for which they had been planning for many, many days. Although American personnel would be merely observers or fringe participants, they could not help but be caught up in all the excitement and euphoria that prevailed throughout the city.

I, the Commanding General of that headquarters referred to as HAC, sat at my desk in the headquarters building. It was readily apparent to me that on this day the concentration level would be low, distractions plentiful, and, consequently, not much that was meaningful would be accomplished. Conceding that this would be the case, I had already decided that I would soon declare this a short work day, a partial holiday, and release all but the normal overnight duty personnel. I knew full well that the streets would be jammed with traffic scarcely moving, so an early departure for my headquarters personnel increased their chances of getting back to their billets before the big celebrating began.

I, like the rest of my people, was upbeat, and I was eagerly looking forward to experiencing this great spectacle, TET, and witnessing what it was all about.

At that moment the phone on my desk rang. As I reached for the receiver to answer it, I had absolutely no clue that in a matter of four or five seconds my world would be unceremoniously turned upside down. I said, "Hello," and the stern, abrupt voice on the other end said, "Irzyk, this is Westmoreland. I have strong indications that sappers may be operating in town tonight. Accordingly, I want your command at maximum alert." Bang! Boom! That was it. So much for the shortened holiday workday. This was certainly a stunning, shocking, totally unexpected development.

Then, without hesitation, my first act was to summon to my office, without delay, Lieutenant Colonels George and Rowe. While awaiting them, I called in key members of my staff. I instructed them to spread the words "maximum alert" to all billets, mess halls and dining facilities, motor pools, engineer compounds, and to all other elements and facilities under the broad HAC umbrella. Furthermore, a high priority and immediate action required the rapid organization of HAC's reaction forces in accordance with plans that had been prepared for just such an emergency. These reaction forces would differ and be over and above those that the MPs would organize.

It was not long before I was huddling with two critically important, very key individuals. Lieutenant Colonel Richard E. George was the commander of the 90th Military Police Detachment. His unit was under my operational command, and provided me with a Provost Marshal capability.

Lieutenant Colonel Gordon D. Rowe was the Commanding Officer of the 716th Military Police Battalion, and he and his unit were also under my operational command. Because of the peculiar situation pertaining in Saigon, it was the largest military police battalion in the entire U.S. Army worldwide. Making him even bigger was the recent attachment to him of the 527th Military Police Company.

Because of mounting tensions in Saigon, I had been augmented with additional personnel who were to be used for security. I had organized them into a Security Guard Company (Provisional). I had placed this HAC unit of 200 men under Rowe's operational command. Thus, his large battalion became even larger with a significant increase in overall capabilities.

As soon as they arrived in my office, I informed them of my brief phone conversation with General Westmoreland, and his terse instructions to me. We got right down to the business at hand. But before discussing details of the situation, each of my visitors got on the phone and issued necessary preliminary instructions to their subordinates. This would instantly get the "wheels rolling." We discussed such matters as converting foot patrols to jeep patrols, having MP reaction forces standing by in complete readiness for an instant move; increasing the manning of some of the most likely targets such as General Westmoreland's MACV Headquarters, HAC headquarters, the Provost Marshal's office, the Armed Forces radio and television station; doubling mobile patrols—there would be forty-one on the streets of Saigon.

When Lieutenant Colonel Rowe returned to his headquarters, he found that his MPs had already ceased to be policemen, and had virtually instantly become warriors. This most dramatic transformation occurred in only a matter of minutes. Most MPs traded in their black, highly lacquered, glossy helmet liners with MP letters on them for steel pots (helmets); their neat, starched, crisp uniforms for fatigues; and their night sticks for automatic weapons, including machine guns. Then they thrust their arms through flak jackets, which they would constantly wear when engaged. What a tremendous turnabout, what an instant change in image—one that would forever be remembered.

Until that steel pot went on his head, the MP in Saigon was anything but a well-liked, respected figure. He was constantly insulted, derided, and called "fuzz" and "fink" by fellow American soldiers. Bar girls hissed, "Numbah ten." But the worst insult frequently thrown at him was "Saigon Warrior." Yes, he was the one who performed the unpopular tasks—checking passes, uniforms, vehicles, and was considered a damper on fun making. But he and his buddies during the previous year were responsible for a fifty-square-mile area of Saigon/Cholon. They met challenges that were as great as those found in any large American city and more. During the previous year, their statistics for Americans were six murders, fifteen suicides, 550 assaults, 1,688 larcenies, 3,767 traffic accidents with eighty-seven fatalities, fifteen thousand curfew, uniform, or pass violations, and the usual scattering of forgery, weapons violations, fraud, black market deals, auto thefts, and morals charges.

Another great transformation, perhaps even more radical, was occurring within the HAC command itself. It is difficult to comprehend, but the enlisted strength of HAC was a mere 628. Amazingly, this was considerably less than the strength of the 716th MP Battalion. All 628 of those individuals performed day-to-day support functions for the command. Some were absolutely essential to the operation of the headquarters, and could not be spared. Others were clerks, cooks, mechanics, drivers. None of these young soldiers had the benefit of any type of tactical unit training, and were led by officers of varied branches of the army—mainly service branches, and only one who had ever been engaged in previous combat.

So it was out of our "hide" that the HAC Quick Reaction Forces (QRFs) were formed. It was essential that they be located at a number of key installations throughout the Saigon metropolitan area. QRF #1, consisting primarily of troop movement specialists and special services personnel, was positioned at the HAC headquarters and headquarters detachment compound near the Tan Son Nhut Air Base. QRF #2, composed of mechanics, drivers, and clerks, would secure the Thu Tho motor pool, HAC's main motor pool located near the Phu Tho Racetrack. QRF #3, also composed of mechanics, drivers, and clerks, would secure the Bien Vuong sub motor pool in downtown Saigon. QRF #4, made up of commissary and subsistence storage specialists, was directed to secure the COFAT Compound in Cholon, site of the only commissary in Vietnam, as well as a large post exchange, a military clothing sales store, the Saigon Area Civilian Personnel Office, and the Air Force-operated post office.

Other smaller QRFs were positioned at the headquarters of USAHAC, and such activities as the post engineer, repair and utility installations, and the Vietnamese regional exchange warehouse. Every effort was made to place a QRF at a key installation or at a location from which it could rapidly be deployed.

What is striking and absolutely unique about these QRFs is that its members were not only without any tactical training, but were simply a collection of individuals. They had never worked together, and certainly were far from being a team. None was a cohesive unit. Now they were facing a totally unexpected, unbelievable, and possibly the ultimate challenge—combat.

It was not very long after they were alerted, that they were gathered together at a pre positioned location to be issued their combat gear—steel helmets, flak jackets, weapons, and live ammunition.

Absolutely, truly amazing—a service support headquarters was now moving to a war footing. Ironically, it would later be learned that quite a number of the members of QRFs lying in their billets nervously geared up for what they did not know, were watching on TV a very exciting war movie.

By late afternoon after several busy and even frenzied hours of activity, it became eerily quiet. There was no more rushing in and out of my office. People seemed to have vanished into the woodwork. I was now quite alone. And now for me began one of a military commander's most difficult periods. It was like a combat commander who had done all he could to get ready for the attack, and now had to sit back and wait for H hour to see how it would unfold. In my case I had thought and thought, discussed and discussed, and thought some more. I had issued orders and instructions that I deemed necessary, appropriate, and sound. This was a situation totally without precedent. Now all I could do was sit back and assume and hope that my trusted subordinates were implementing my orders and instructions, as directed, and that I would soon receive reports that all was ready to meet the challenge, whatever it might be.

Terrorist attacks in Saigon had become quite common. We had them almost every week. Most were hit and run—a grenade lobbed into a gathering, small arms fire from cars that sped through the streets and on into the night, a grenade fixed to the accelerator of an American jeep by a young teenager that exploded and killed when the driver's foot pressed the accelerator. The terrorist attacks came in a wide variety of packages. Yet, it was extremely rare to receive even a very small, concentrated attack. On occasion we received information that terrorist activity might take place. To be ready on those occasions, alerts were called and appropriate orders issued. The men would appropriately gear up, and often nothing would happen, so they had become a bit jaded. On this day when they went to maximum alert, the feeling most probably was, "Okay, here we go again." That night when they retired, some MPs may have done so with not too great a feeling of trepidation.

As I sat, I could not help but keep wondering about what it was that might happen. Would all this hectic activity and the preparations turn out to be unnecessary, a "dry run?" Or, would my command be actively engaged? If so, in what manner? Would it be something easily handled, or something worse than imagined, perhaps something even quite drastic? Whatever it turned out to be—were we ready?

As I continued my reflections, I could not help but remember the date of December 15, 1967, just a month and a half before, when General Westmoreland made a surprising decision. As a result of that decision, which exemplified the relaxed mood in Saigon, the battle for Saigon was almost lost before it ever began. Because of the U.S. relationship with, and the sensibilities of, the Army of the Republic of Vietnam (ARVN), General Westmoreland on that date turned over full responsibility for the defense of Saigon to the ARVN.

Thus, on January 31, 1968, unless individuals were passing through or were there on temporary duty, there were no U.S. tactical troops within the city of Saigon.

On January 31, 1968 there was no U.S. tactical headquarters in Saigon.

I was fully aware that on this day in Saigon, as was the case all over the country, the ranks of the ARVN military would be radically depleted. TET tradition called for as many individuals as possible to return to their homes for the holidays. This custom applied fully as well to their armed forces. So, as I sat at my desk, I was not the least bit comfortable realizing that there was not, in Saigon, a single American tactical trooper, or an American tactical headquarters with all its combat resources, and that those ARVN units in town were dangerously under strength. Since there was nothing else, I knew without question that the security responsibility for Saigon had slipped in my direction, and more than ever sat squarely upon my shoulders.

Although my headquarters did not have an intelligence gathering capability that did not mean that I was unaware of what was going on outside of Saigon. On the contrary, I believe that overall, I was nearly as well informed as most anyone in the theater. I, or my chief of staff, regularly attended meetings at MACV headquarters. During those meetings, attended by persons with high security clearances, I heard firsthand reports, presentations, discussions that kept me fully abreast of such important items as current intelligence and military and civic operations that were taking place throughout the country. Periodically, as the so called "Military Mayor of Saigon," I would be asked pertinent questions about the city, and often was asked to give my assessment of the "goings on" in the capital city. After the meetings, I often discussed matters, one on one, with senior members of the MACV staff.

Each Saturday afternoon, I would drive to Long Binh to meet with my other commander, the Commanding General, U.S. Army, Vietnam, Lieutenant General Bruce Palmer. I would sit at a table with members of his staff and other commanders, and our discussions would be comprehensive and long ranging. Based on those meetings and the ones at MACV, I knew what was going on.

Still in my chair, I continued to ponder about information that

I had picked up during recent weeks. It moved me from being uneasy to quite disturbed. I was well aware that journalists, who also had good sources, had begun to believe that something big might be happening soon. Because of this, several news agencies were at full alert, and some even went so far as to cancel R&R (rest and recuperation) for some journalists, so as to have them ready for the big enemy push if it came.

Adding weight to this information, there were reports that enemy documents in large numbers had been captured and were circulated—an important one as recently as November 19. From the enemy documents there appeared to be evidence of their intentions, but no indication that their capabilities were anywhere close to matching those intentions.

By December 1967 high-ranking American officers began to believe that the Communists would try a major offensive in the near future. Evidence of this was demonstrated by the highest military officer of them all, General Earle Wheeler, Chairman of the Joint Chiefs of Staff. He made an address to an American public audience on December 18 in which he issued a warning that such an attack could take place. Wheeler based his warning on an analysis prepared by Westmoreland and his staff. Ironically, it is safe to assume that on the day he was delivering his remarks, General Wheeler was surely not thinking back to the cataclysmic event that had taken place, almost to the day, twenty-three years before.

It was on December 16, 1944 that the great German surprise attack erupted in the Ardennes—Belgium and Luxembourg—that became the "Battle of the Bulge." Little did he realize, as he spoke, that a similar intelligence failure and another staggering enemy surprise would occur in just a month and a half. History often plays great and puzzling tricks, and it did for me. I was very much on the scene for both of those intelligence failures. My unit and I bitterly fought in that first battle in December 1944, and my command and I would soon be heavily engaged in the second, during January /February 1968. Two of my battles, twenty-three years apart, would result from unforgiving intelligence breakdowns.

Despite all the disquieting information floating around during the weeks before TET, General Westmoreland was of the opinion that certain U.S. units around Saigon had become less essential. The enemy had been pushed back toward Cambodia, and Westmoreland planned to use the released units from the Saigon area to reinforce planned and quite massive search and destroy operations scheduled to begin along the Cambodian border in early 1968.

On what turned out to be quite a fateful day, January 10, 1968, Lieutenant General Fred Weyand, Commanding General, II Field Force, Vietnam, met with General Westmoreland at MACV Headquarters. General Weyand's operational responsibilities for Saigon were restricted to approaches to the city. On that day he presented intelligence that indicated that even as U.S. operations began on the Cambodian border, the enemy forces were infiltrating in the direction of Saigon. Weyand feared that an attack of some kind was in the making. He stressed to Westmoreland that the Viet Cong had been maneuvering in large units with reinforcements of North Vietnamese and with new weapons. He asked that the border operations be postponed, and that certain U.S. units be returned to their positions in the populated areas near Saigon.

General Westmoreland initially resisted Weyand's opinions and entreaties, but then relented and agreed. As a result of that decision, by the time TET broke twenty-seven combat battalions were back in the Saigon circle, a forty-five kilometer circle around Saigon.

As events would later unfold, that decision would turn out to be not only extraordinarily critical and important with many ramifications, but would be instrumental in helping save Saigon.

I had sat at my desk for quite some time. During my reflections, I had remained undisturbed, an absolute rarity. I shook myself, and realized once again that it was apparent that I had done all I could—for the moment there was nothing more for me to do. From long experience I knew that an effective commander, once an operation is underway and because it is always in short supply, takes every opportunity to grab some rest. I decided to do just that. I first walked into the operations area, learned that all was in place, and found nothing unusual happening. I talked to the personnel who had duty that night. We kicked around the various types of activity that we might expect, and the measures we would take to respond to them. We did not have many experience factors to compare. After all, as mentioned, during the previous year, terrorist attacks were scattered, "hit and run." They had not been organized enough to cause the 716th Battalion any serious casualties. The 716th MP Battalion had lost no men in the line of duty.

I was satisfied that the night duty team was "with the program." I called for my driver and car, and we headed for my residence in the heart of downtown Saigon. For a brief moment I wondered if I was up to bucking the traffic that would be out there. I quickly decided that my bed at home was preferable to my cot in the office, and that it would be worth the fight to get home.

For the first few minutes we made slow but steady progress, but the closer we edged to downtown Saigon, the more difficult it became. It was not long before difficult became impossible. The broad streets and sidewalks were tightly jammed with people—hundreds of people, thousands of people on foot—shouting, singing, dancing, swaying, hugging. Swallowed up and clogged by the mass of humanity were bicycles, motorcycles, pedicabs, small cars, and my car. Each of those edged forward slowly, gingerly, as the crowd pressed ahead like a writhing serpent. Every few moments an individual would shove aside his companions, make a little hole, wave through a vehicle, only to have the gap quickly close. All the while, firecrackers were crackling—exploding noisily, constantly, incessantly, and bouncing crazily in all directions.

It was incredible, absolutely one of a kind, none anywhere else like it—a sight never before experienced and never to be forgotten.

Miraculously, with patience and aggressive maneuvering, my driver had somehow reached and fought his way into my driveway. We were home. As I walked into my quarters, much to my surprise the phone was silent and would remain that way.

After a quick bite to eat, as customary, I laid out at the ready a fresh uniform for the next day. Since it had been a demanding and exhausting day, and not knowing what the night or next day might bring, I decided to "hit the hay." Despite the tumult, the booming, crackling, shouting—noise many decibels higher than any I had ever experienced—I somehow fell asleep.

HAC AT WAR

CHAPTER 7
HAC AT WAR

It seemed that I had been asleep for but minutes when I came bolt upright in my bed. Loud, booming, reverberating, frightening explosions had abruptly and rudely awakened me, and figuratively blew me out of my bed. I was standing completely awake, but surprised, shaken, and shocked, and trying to comprehend what it was that was happening out there. "Out there" was close, very close—could not have been more than five or six blocks from where I resided in downtown Saigon.

I glanced at my watch, which read 2:47 A.M. I furiously began dressing in the clothes that I had laid out for just such an emergency.

What was occurring most certainly was not "sappers in town," which General Westmoreland had warned me about. No, this was something much, much bigger—something really *big*!

I was dressed in what appeared to be but an instant. I dashed out the door. Fast as I had been, Sergeant Williams was faster. My six foot, five inch military police driver and bodyguard was standing fully dressed with the car doors open and the engine idling. There was only one place for me now, and it was my headquarters. Williams, of course, knew. I simply nodded to him, and without a word we both jumped in, and the car was instantly backing out of the driveway as we slammed the doors shut, and then moved out onto the street.

Just a handful of hours before, we had to fight foot by foot to get home. Now there was nothing, absolutely nothing, only total darkness and absolute silence. Astonishing! Incredible! Unbelievable!

Once on the street, we turned and headed for the headquarters. It was perfectly obvious that something was wrong, terribly wrong. My first thought was, "What happened to all the people?"

When I slipped into bed just a few hours earlier, the streets were jammed, a teeming mass of humanity. Pedicabs, taxis, and cars were stopped cold, barely able to move. Even individuals on foot were having difficulty pushing their way along. On that day, January 30, the first and most holy day of TET, the Lunar New Year, the city of Saigon was celebrating, and that night was the peak of that celebration. Everyone was a reveler—singing, dancing, laughing, shouting, screaming. Firecrackers were popping, snapping, bouncing in endless strings, everywhere.

Now it was January 31, and as my car picked up speed, unbelievably, incredibly, the streets were deathly still. Not a single soul of Saigon's three million people was visible, not one. It was eerie, uncanny, breathtaking, mystifying. The sudden, remarkable contrast was unimaginable, most difficult, virtually impossible to comprehend. It was as though a plague had suddenly hit the city, and wiped it out in one fell swoop, or a huge swarm of giant locusts had consumed the entire populace.

My car was not moving at the usual, slow, tortuous pace. Anything but. It was racing along Saigon streets at sixty miles per hour, yes sixty miles per hour. *In Saigon's long history it is safe to say that no other car has ever traversed its streets at such speed.*

Ah, but there was life out there, somewhere in the darkness. Scattered, random rifle shots—definitely not firecrackers—were aimed at my speeding car, but fell harmlessly behind it.

What was normally a slow, often frustrating, time consuming trip, now seemed to take but an instant. The car slowed as it approached a large sign that read, UNITED STATES ARMY HEADQUARTERS AREA COMMAND, my headquarters.

The security guard recognized my car immediately, opened the gate, and waved me through. I rushed into the building, raced up the stairs, and into the duty officer's room, the operations room. Pandemonium! He and his augmented staff were frantically at work. Every phone within sight and sound was ringing incessantly, demanding to be answered. There just were not enough hands, arms, ears.

The minute he noted my presence, the Duty Officer rushed up to me. His first words were, "Sir, our Embassy is under attack. Our MPs have been dispatched and are rushing to it."

The 1968 TET attack on Saigon was furiously unfolding.

I could not believe what I was hearing and seeing. This was not the quiet, business like room with which I was familiar. It had, in an instant, become a war room. Every one of the phone conversations concerned *enemy* activity, *enemy* attacks.

Forget my service support missions, now a *war* was being fought out there. For the next many hours, HAC's assigned "Specific Functions and Responsibilities" that went from A to Y were figuratively being shot to pieces. HAC now had but one "Function and Responsibility"—fight furiously with all the resources it could muster, and operate selflessly to save every possible individual and installation for which it was responsible, until the tactical troops arrived to bring reinforcements to assist and then take over the battle.

As the calls came in, staff members were furiously attempting to make a record of them. The log for January 31 was fast developing. However, the calls for help by radio and phone came in so rapidly that it was difficult to post them all. Only about a quarter of the calls were able to be recorded. A sampling of the calls that did make it into the log are listed here, and they only hint at the magnitude, extent, intensity, and horror of enemy actions throughout the city during the first hours of the TET offensive.

0246 U.S. Embassy under attack.

0300 Bachelor Officers Quarters #3 (major military housing compound for senior officers, including general officers) attacked savagely.

0300 Simultaneous attack on adjacent Vietnamese Joint General Staff Headquarters.

0316 Explosion at Phoenix City, Bachelor Enlisted Quarters.

0317 Explosion at Town House BOQ.

0318 BOQ #1 under attack.

0319 MacArthur BOQ under attack.

0321 Report of attack at Rex Hotel (major hotel).

0325 Explosion at BOQ #2.

0340 Automatic weapons fire and continued attack at BOQ #3.

0341 MPs at U.S. Embassy request urgent ammunition supply.

0342 Heavy sniper fire at Metropole BEQ.

0350 Incoming mortars at Montana BEQ.

0358 Saigon Port area reports small arms and automatic weapons fire.

0359 Mortar and rocket fire at U.S. Embassy; reinforcements requested.

0400 Enemy fire received at HAC motor pool.

0407 MP jeep C9A reports that a 2-and-a-half ton truck carrying a twenty-five man reaction force on way to BOQ #3 is hit by rockets and claymore mines. Heavy casualties.

0408 Jeep C9A hit; both MPs killed.

0419 BOQ #3 pleads for ammunition re-supply.

0420 Cleveland and Columbia BEQs request ammunition and assistance.

0420 General Westmoreland calls; orders first priority effort to recapture the U.S. Embassy. (It had not been captured.)

0430 Request armored vehicles and helicopters from tactical units for Embassy assault.

0449 Repeat. Cleveland and Columbia BEQs require ammunition and assistance.

0500 Three Claymores detonated at the Saigon motor pool. Booby traps discovered.

0516 Explosions and small arms fire at Royal Oaks BEQ.

0535 Automatic weapons fire at Butte BEQ.

0542 MP shot in attack on Denbigh BOQ.

0546 Claymore detonated at Flint BOQ.
0600 Camp Red Ball under attack.
0602 MP machine gun jeep captured by Viet Cong.
0613 Claymores detonated at several BOQs.
0615 Area near Ambassador Bunkers' home hit by mortars and automatic weapons fire.

As is perfectly obvious from the log just described, chaos reigned supreme in Saigon. The city was brought to a standstill. Virtually all movement had ceased. Individuals of every stripe and station were frightened, confused, terrified, frantic, frustrated. They were forcibly restricted to their billets, and feared for their safety. They feared leaving their billets even more. There were cases early on when inhabitants of billets, without steel helmets or flak jackets and armed only with pistols, came out firing when the VC threatened their billets.

Very many individuals absolutely needed to get to their places of work, but could not without armed escorts. These were hard to come by as such guards had a higher priority mission—fighting VC. Generals and senior diplomats not only needed but demanded armed escorts, but under such circumstances, they too had to be left high and dry.

Newspaper and TV personnel were particularly torn, frantic, and frustrated. There were huge stories out there, everywhere, begging to be reported upon. They, too, demanded armed escorts, and when unable to obtain them, many took great risks by grabbing any stray vehicle that they could get their hands on.

As for the Vietnamese, there were absolutely no sightings or movement. For the hundreds of thousands of Vietnamese in Saigon from the moment of the first shot fired, there had not been visible a single light, sound, face, peep, or move. Families were tightly holed up in their mostly very tiny homes. As the hours passed, they would be faced with shortages of food and water. Survival would become a new and desperate challenge.

The only known exception to the tightly confined Vietnamese was certain members of the HAC security guards. About a third of the force seemingly and, miraculously, popped up out of nowhere to courageously occupy their posts. I had always been proud of the loyalty of our HAC work force. There could be no better example of loyalty than that shown by our security guards during those first difficult hours.

It was not only the Vietnamese who were forced to tighten their belts; all Americans and members of foreign governments were faced with a gradual depletion of life's necessities. Mess sergeants were eager to get to their dining facilities, but were not able to. Even if they had been successful, producing food was out of the question. They could not procure trucks. Even if they had trucks, it would not have been possible for them to get them safely to the supply points. And, of course, at the supply points there would have been no one to issue the rations. It would take many hours for all elements of the "system" to be safely back in action.

Ironically, of all things, senior Vietnamese military and diplomatic officials, as well as senior Americans, would be in constant touch with HAC to obtain from that headquarters information about what was happening in their city. It was readily obvious that they did not have available, or could not rely on, their normal sources.

What is especially disturbing, MACV, General Westmoreland's headquarters, not only had a battle going on in Saigon, but a war raging countrywide. MACV for a time was handicapped, and not able to get a complete handle on things.

There is no better example or more graphic evidence of how chaotic, confusing, desperate, and dangerous Saigon had instantly become, than to describe the situation in which General Abrams found himself. General Creighton Abrams was the deputy to General Westmoreland (and would later succeed him). At this time, Abrams was the number two U.S. military man in Vietnam. His concerns and responsibilities were countrywide. Yet, he was unable, at the most crucial time, to reach his headquarters, to get to his desk, but most importantly to reach his communications, so as to be able to assess the situation, and to take needed action. Momentarily, he was powerless.

Rather than occupying a villa in downtown Saigon, along with other dignitaries, he purposely selected much more modest quarters that located him very near Tan Son Nhut and MACV. Yet, for some hours he, too, was a prisoner in his own home.

When all hell broke loose in Saigon, he immediately contacted the MACV command center. He was informed that heavy attacks were being initiated throughout the city and nationwide, as well, but that no major patterns had as yet been determined. Based on this paucity of information, he knew that he had to get to his headquarters. He called for an escort to protect his vehicle so that he could move out. He was bluntly told to stay put, that enemy elements were operating between his home and his headquarters, and that it was too dangerous at the time to attempt even the short drive to MACV.

An awkward situation complicated matters. He had as his houseguest an individual who ironically had arrived to assess the situation in Vietnam. He was General Bruce C. Clarke, who had been Abrams' combat commander during WW II, and had risen to the rank of four-star general as Commanding General, U.S. Army Europe. (I, who was also a member of that division, had spent an evening at General Abrams' quarters with those two individuals just prior to the TET attack.)

It was not until later in the day that Abrams was able to get out, and under heavy escort made it safely to his headquarters. Once there, he grasped eagerly and desperately for information so that he could analyze the situation and take the necessary action required. What aggravated the situation and made matters even more critical for General Abrams and MACV was that the Newport Hotel in Saigon, which housed many vitally important members of the large MACV staff of radio operators, clerks, and intelligent specialists, was under attack. This prevented those critically needed individuals from making it safely to MACV.

A most frightening and disturbing element about this situation was that because of the confusion and chaos in Saigon, at the highest military level there appeared to be no awareness, no accurate, professional assessment of what was transpiring in Saigon and the rest of the country. For an initial period there appeared to be no hands exerting control or direction.

Frustration piled upon frustration. General Abrams learned that he could not get back to his quarters. Late that evening the few senior generals who had somehow managed to reach MACV assembled in a makeshift dining room for an evening meal. This was a first. Until now, MACV had no requirement for, and thus had no mess facility for, 'round the clock operations.

As they sat around the table, the mood was extremely gloomy. To emphasize the frustrating and chaotic situation, a stray bullet smashed a window of the room in which the generals were eating. How humiliating, humbling, inglorious. "Pentagon East" had now been violated. The generals, of course, made a hasty exit to another room.

General Abrams was not able to leave the headquarters until the next day, when a helicopter hastily plucked him from the ground. That was approximately thirty-two hours after the first enemy shot had been fired in the city. Certainly, a graphic picture of chaotic Saigon.

PITCHED BATTLES AND ENGAGEMENTS

CHAPTER 8
THE EMBASSY FIGHT

Just three months earlier, the 2.6 million dollar Embassy Compound had been completed and opened on Thong Nhut Street. Its six-story chancery building loomed over Saigon like an impregnable fortress. The building was a white reinforced concrete complex. It was encased in a massive concrete sunscreen that overlapped shatterproof Plexiglas windows, and was protected by a sturdy ten-foot high concrete wall.

It was a constant reminder to all who saw it of the power and prestige of America. It was a massive structure. But its symbolism was even more enormous. It goes without saying that the Embassy was, for the Communists, an absolutely huge target, the prime target in Saigon, and without a doubt in all of Vietnam as well. Seizing the U.S. Embassy quickly was a vital, critical mission for the Communists. They astutely recognized the tremendous symbolic and psychological effect that the triumph of hoisting and flying the Communist flag over the U.S. Embassy within minutes of their push into Saigon would have. There would be worldwide reverberations. Consequently, during the very first minutes of the Communist assault on Saigon, the American Embassy was the prime target of the initial, important installations to be attacked and seized.

It was a small force of sappers—only twenty individuals—who had the mission, did the attacking. The sappers belonged to a very special breed. They were little people who were devious, dangerous, lethal. They were able to slither under coiled barbed wire protecting

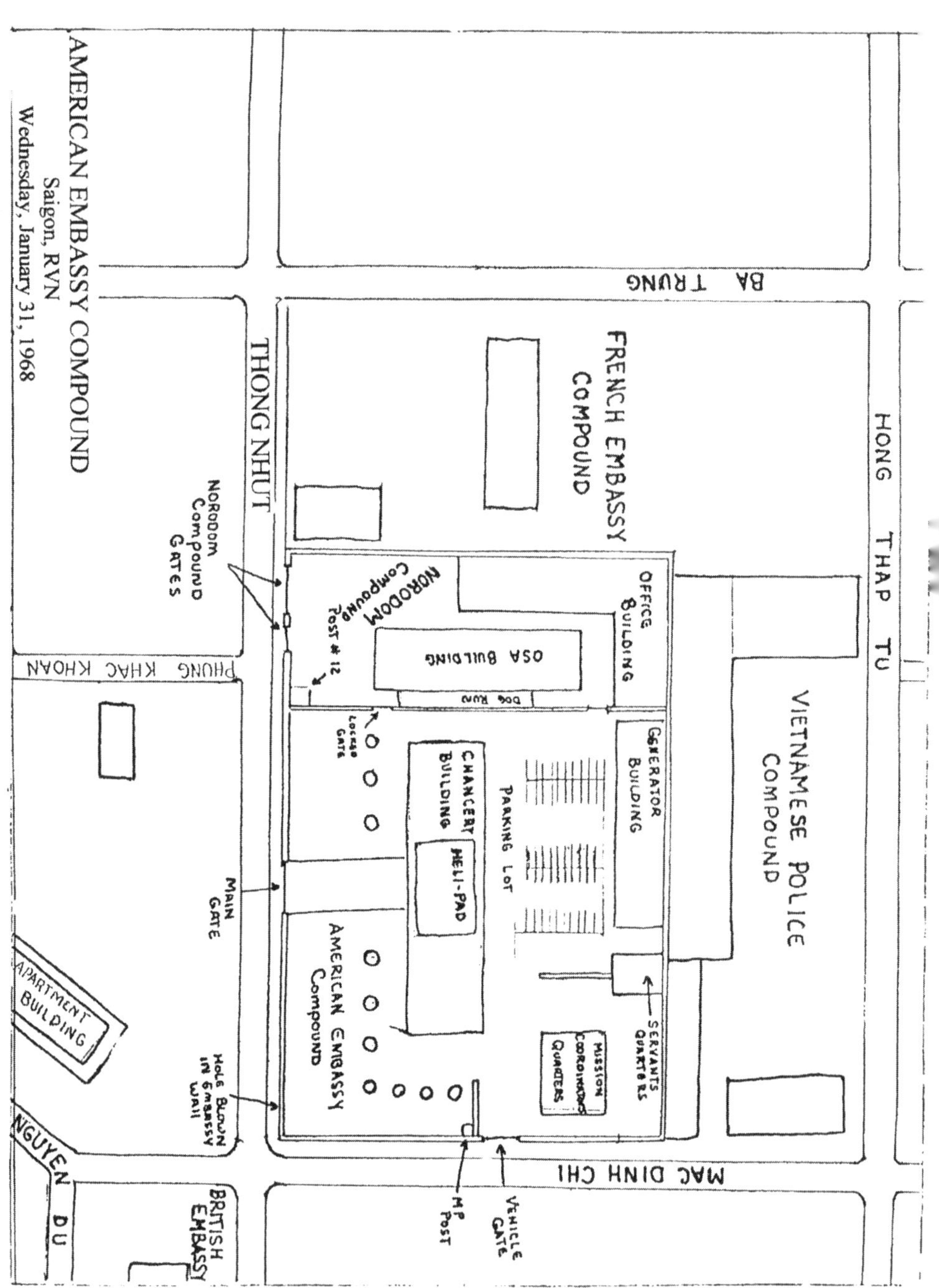

American Embassy Compound, Saigon, RVN, Wednesday, January 31, 1968.

American firebases without disturbing Claymore mines, and wreak havoc within the firebase. Their missions, which they willingly accepted, were habitually suicide missions. Thus, their selection for the Embassy assault, they recognized, could be a suicide mission, and they were well prepared for it.

Twenty men, at first blush, would appear to be a very small force entrusted with such a valuable and formidable objective. However, as we are well aware, the sappers expected little or no resistance from ARVN forces. The Vietnamese police force, responsible for the exterior security of the Embassy, was a corrupt organization, and anything but courageous, so they were definitely not a threat. Understandably, the sappers believed that they had nothing to fear from the Vietnamese. That left them to deal with the members of the U.S. Marine Security Detachment (MSD) assigned to the Embassy, who were responsible for its security. However, that was a very small force, which was lightly armed.

On the other hand, twenty men, banded together, moving aggressively about the tight confines of the Embassy grounds, would quickly become a crowd. That small crowd, armed with AK-47s, B-40 Rocket Propelled Grenades (RPGs), and satchel charges, would quickly become a small, extremely potent army.

Sometime after midnight, and before the VC opened their attack on Saigon, the sappers met with their two team leaders. Those individuals outlined the plan and issued instructions. It was a simple operation. The sappers were to scale the wall and seize control of the chancery. No withdrawal plan was mentioned.

The meeting took place only five blocks from the Embassy at a greasy car repair shop and garage at 59 Phan Than Gian Street. At the appointed time those twenty VC sappers climbed into a small Peugeot truck and a taxicab for the short ride to their objective, the U.S. Embassy. They wore black pajamas and shirts, much like ordinary civilians, and red armbands. This Embassy team came from the elite 250-man-strong C10 Sapper Battalion, whose headquarters was near the Michelin rubber plantation north of Saigon. Some of these individuals had been born in Saigon and were familiar with the streets of the crowded city, had worked there as taxi and pedicab drivers. Others arrived on busses packed with holiday travelers two days before the TET attack, and went to safe houses—some next door to the repair shop. It was at this location where their weapons and explosives had been smuggled in over the previous weeks in rented trucks loaded with rice, tomatoes, and firewood, and stashed.

The Embassy sappers rendezvoused with their team leaders at the repair shop and the cached weapons were broken out of their containers. Their assault on the Embassy would be only a part of the sapper battalion's assignment, which was to spearhead the attack on Saigon followed closely by eleven battalions of VC, totaling about four thousand troops.

The battalion's mission that morning, in addition to seizing the U.S. Embassy, was to gain control of the Presidential Palace, the national broadcasting studio, the South Vietnamese Naval Headquarters, the Vietnamese Joint General Staff headquarters at the Tan Son Nhut Airbase, and the Philippine Embassy. All of these were to be held by the sappers for forty-eight hours until the VC battalions pouring into the city would relieve them.

Immediately after the word was out that the U.S. Embassy was being assaulted, shockwaves quickly circled the globe. The astonishing news was grave, frightening, and caused great consternation for much of America. Heretofore, the folks at home did not appear unduly upset, and were taking the war pretty much in stride. It was difficult to follow engagements that were taking place half a world away. They found that the attacks, the battles, and the places in Vietnam were unpronounceable, the type of war and locations were, for them, quite vague. So for most Americans, the fight at the Embassy was at last something very real. That engagement was the first tangible battle of the Vietnam War, which they understood, was simple, and clear. Yes, it was a dramatic eye-opener.

The U.S. Embassy, Saigon, Vietnam
The early morning hours of January 31, 1968

Like members of the Headquarters Area Command (HAC), the U.S. Marine Security Guard Detachment (MSG), was at a heightened alert and readiness. Captain Robert J. O'Brien, the officer in charge of the MSG detachments, had met with Mr. Leo Campsey, the State Department regional security officer, at 1600 the previous afternoon, and was informed of the possibility of a sapper attack in the Saigon area. In response to this information Captain O'Brien directed that a second guard would be posted at all one-man posts, and that a rooftop watch be established at the new chancery building at the U.S. Embassy.

At 0100 hours Marine Sergeant Raymond P. Schuepfer and Lance Corporal James P. Wilson assumed their duties at Guard Post #12 in the Norodom Compound, across the interior wall separating it from the chancery building. Additionally, Sergeant Schuepfer had been designated as the walking, roving patrol, responsible for checking the area on an hourly basis.

At 0200 hours Marine Sergeant Ronald W. Harper, who had assumed duties at the important and very critical Guard Post #1, which was the lobby and front desk of the chancery building, along with Corporal Zahuranic, decided to go to the roof of the building to relieve the previously posted Sergeant Rudy A. Soto for a short break.

While on the roof, Sergeant Harper looked out in all directions, in and around the Embassy. He spotted nothing unusual, and all appeared normal and quiet. Sergeant Soto completed his break at 0215 hours, and returned to his post on the roof. With that Sergeant Harper moved out and began his descent to his post in the lobby.

Shortly after, at 0238 Sergeant Harper again left Post #1 to see if his guards at Post #12 in the Norodom Compound needed coffee. As he approached the post, he met Sergeant Schuepfer, who was returning from his patrol of the compound, and reported that all was quiet. As Sergeant Harper was pouring a cup of coffee, he glanced toward the office building and observed a Vietnamese man standing nearby. As Harper was about to ask if the individual was an Embassy guard or driver, the man raised a weapon and automatic fire came spewing forth. As he recoiled in surprise, Sergeant Harper heard, from a different direction, a deafening explosion that must have come from someplace very close. He dropped his cup and rushed from the guard shack at the dead run, heading for his own post. There was no sign of the armed Vietnamese, who had somehow disappeared. As he ran, Sergeant Harper was completely unaware of the action taking place not much more than a stone's throw away.

Two Military Policemen occupied a post at the side gate of the Embassy on Mac Dinh Chi. The front main gate facing Thong Nhut had been secured for the night, but the side gate remained unlocked. At this time a small truck and taxi with their lights off moved silently along Mac Dinh Chi. They moved past a Vietnamese police station and an officer-occupied checkpoint. However, there was absolutely no reaction from the Vietnamese police. Upon reaching Thong Nhut, the sappers turned right on that street. As they did, fire from an AK-47 came out of their taxi aimed at the two MPs standing at their post at the side gate. The vehicles continued slowly down the road and were out of sight. The moment the vehicles stopped, the sappers were out, and instantly began unloading their RPGs and satchel charges from the vehicles.

The two MPs had earlier been issued steel helmets and flak-jackets and had them on when they occupied their post. They were Specialist Four Charles L. Daniel and Private First Class William E. Sebast of the 527th MP Company, which had been attached to the 716th MP Battalion. At the sound of the first AK-47 shots, without hesitation both MPs dashed inside the Embassy Compound, slammed the steel barred door with a loud clang, and locked it with the heavy chain and padlock.

Events were now moving swiftly. It was now 0247. Less than ten minutes earlier, Sergeant Harper had been at Post #12 checking to see if his guards needed coffee.

Specialist Four Daniel's next action was to grab his guard post radio, which, of course, was on the MP network. He shouted, "WACO, WACO, this is the American Embassy!" and added, "Signal 300," which was the brief code for enemy attack. (This report is what my driver, Sergeant Williams, heard in his quarters behind mine, as he always had his MP radio on. The moment he heard the report he began to dress furiously.) Daniel had barely finished his message when he and Sebast were literally rocked back on their heels and deafened by the noise of a powerful explosion. As soon as they were able to settle themselves, they saw that sappers had blown a hole in the southeast corner of the ten-foot wall. (It was this explosion that had rudely awakened me at my quarters only a few blocks away. My watch read 0247.) The hole initially was relatively small, but so were the sappers. The hole was large enough for the tiny sappers to wiggle and crawl through.

Daniel and Sebast immediately grabbed their M-16s, swung their weapons so that the muzzles pointed straight toward the hole, and sprayed it with multiple rounds from their guns. The two sappers already through the hole were instantly killed. Firing AK-47s ahead of them, the VC continued to penetrate the hole while others scaled the wall. Soon they were pouring out a very heavy volume of AK-47 fire. Most unfortunately, regrettably, and tragically, Daniel and Sebast were overwhelmed, and never had a chance. Daniel was shot in the face and Sebast in the chest, and both died instantly. Their crumbled bodies were soon covered with concrete fragments and dust, as the barrage of AK-47 fire splintered the wall behind them. As the dead MPs lay facedown on the ground, the sappers began fanning out over the Embassy grounds.

At a dead run, after leaving Post #12, Sergeant Harper reached the front door of the chancery and quickly darted inside. He, at that point, was unaware of the events that had unfolded around the corner near the vehicle gate; that the explosion he had heard had blasted a hole in the Embassy wall. Once inside the chancery, he immediately locked the main door. As he was doing that, two sappers positioned themselves behind a circular concrete planter. One quickly aimed his RPG at the front door of the chancery. Just as Sergeant Harper turned away from the door, a B-40 rocket exploded against that six-inch teakwood main door, sending shrapnel into the lobby. One bit of shrapnel entered Harper's leg. Corporal Zahuranic was not as fortunate. He had been sitting at the receptionist desk talking to Mr. E. Allen Wendt, the Embassy Duty Officer.

Zahuranic received a serious shrapnel wound to the head resulting in severe bleeding from his head and ear. He also suffered a broken leg.

As Sergeant Harper was applying first aid to the unconscious Zahuranic, a second B-40 rocket was fired, penetrated the granite slab bearing the seal of the United States, and exploded near the receptionist desk. Neither Harper nor Zahuranic was further injured by that blast.

As earlier mentioned, Sergeant Soto was positioned on the roof of the chancery. He had heard an explosion coming from the direction of the Presidential Palace. He immediately moved along the roof to the edge so as to be able to see better. As he looked down, he saw Vietnamese running toward the Embassy, and after they reached the high wall he watched in horror as a blast opened a hole in that wall at the corner of Mac Dinh Chi and Thong Nhut. Almost immediately, he heard automatic fire, and picked out the first defenders of the Embassy Compound: Daniel and Sebast holding their ground and pouring accurate fire at the break in the wall, killing two sappers before being cut down themselves. Their courageous and valiant stand provided the split second timing that Sergeant Harper had required to rush to the front entrance of the chancery and to secure its main door. Unquestionably, the VC would have rushed into the building if it were not for Daniel and Sebast's gallant action.

It was ironic and tragic that Sergeant Soto was able to observe all this action, but was unable to help the besieged MPs. He was armed only with a shotgun and .38 pistol. With his shotgun he attempted to provide supporting fire, but his shotgun jammed twice while he was chambering a round. His .38 was way out of range and, thus, was useless.

The noise at the Embassy was heard five blocks away at the Security Guard billet, a converted hotel known as the Marine House. Captain O'Brien, the officer in charge of the Marine security guards, had only recently returned from a tour of his detachment's posts. Now he, accompanied by a sergeant, rushed to his radio-equipped sedan, and headed right for the Embassy. Three other Marines followed in an International Scout. The Marine Security Guards wore their regular utilities (fatigues) and caps. They were not able to convert to infantry as the MPs had and, thus, did not wear steel helmets or flak jackets. At the intersection of Mac Dinh Chi and Hong Thap Tu was a Vietnamese checkpoint. For the very first time that evening they finally "showed themselves" by pointing in the direction of the Embassy, and shouting, "VC! VC!"

Captain O'Brien had his little team dismount from their vehicles, and advance on foot to the locked vehicle gate, right next to the Daniel/Sebast post where it all began. When he reached the locked gate, in hushed tones he tried to make contact with the two MPs. Puzzled, he, of course, received no response.

At that moment Captain O'Brien was unaware that a very real war had begun. Within seconds of one another, men on both sides had been killed in action near where he was now standing. Daniel and Sebast and the two sappers, if not the first, were certainly among the earliest casualties of that war in Saigon. And as Captain O'Brien would soon learn, two of his Marines had already been wounded at that most critically important location, Post #1.

Alerted by his movement, six sappers inside the compound spun toward the Marines on the outside, and suddenly O'Brien was face to face with that war. Now there was an eyeball-to-eyeball confrontation. O'Brien's only weapon was a pistol, so he shouted to one of his sergeants who had a Beretta, and who instantly shoved the muzzle of his submachine gun through the barred gate and without hesitation sent forth a burst. He scored a hit, for he watched as a sapper fell to the ground. That was the first Marine-inflicted casualty. The remaining sappers retaliated by sending forth a heavy volume of fire, which forced the lightly armed Marines back across the street. There they tried to take cover behind trees, and futilely fired their pistols. This was no contest—small arms fire versus automatic weapons fire from the enemy.

Marine Staff Sergeant Leroy J. Banks was also awakened by the explosions at the Embassy. He dressed quickly and rushed to the front gate of the Marine House, where he assumed command of the reaction force that had assembled there.

He moved out with his reaction force within minutes of Captain O'Brien, and headed for the front side of the Embassy. As they advanced, Banks split his little force into two teams—one to move along the roadway trees and the other to follow him along the front wall of the Embassy.

From the already alarmingly busy MP net, Lieutenant Colonel George, the Provost Marshal, was quickly aware of the attack upon the Embassy. His first action was to direct the 716th Military Police Battalion to respond to the attack by sending a reaction force to the Embassy. As part of his instructions, he reminded the force to dismount a block away, and to check out the situation on foot.

It was Sergeant Leslie R. Trent, the Charge of Quarters, 527th Military Police Company, who rushed to Sergeant Rivera's room in the International Hotel, and told him to get his reaction force moving as the American Embassy was under attack. Since they had slept in their fatigues, it took Rivera only a matter of minutes to form his team. At the same time, what little information was available was being passed on to Lieutenant Frank Ribich by his battalion commander, Lieutenant Colonel Rowe. It would be Ribich who would take charge of the reaction force. Sergeant Rivera had, in the meantime, moved his men to the alert vehicles.

As this was taking place, back at the Embassy, Sergeant Bank's reaction force, upon nearing the Norodom Compound, came under heavy automatic fire. Banks yelled to Sergeant Schuepfer, who was inside, to unlock the gate. Banks was told that that there were already sappers inside the main Embassy Compound. Banks immediately decided to let his men, who were under the cover of the tree line, remain there while his fire team moved up along the wall to the main gate, where they could fire through the wrought-iron gate into the compound. As they moved along the wall toward the compound, a hand grenade was tossed over the wall, hitting Sergeant James W. Jimerson on the leg. He reacted instantly, kicked the grenade into the road, and yelled to his buddies, "Hit the deck!" which they did.

That saved them, for although the grenade exploded, none were injured. Almost instantly, the group came under heavy sniper fire and another tossed grenade came over the wall. They were forced to retrace their steps to the Norodom gate. This time Sergeant Banks and his reaction team were able to move inside through the gate, which Sergeant Schuepfer had unlocked for them.

Back at the International Hotel, Lieutenant Ribich joined Sergeant Rivera, and they loaded their reaction force into the waiting vehicles. These consisted of a three-quarter-ton truck and a jeep. Each member of the force was armed with a .45 caliber pistol with three magazines of .45 caliber ammunition, and an M-16 rifle with a hundred rounds of ammunition. Once loaded, the reaction force departed for the John F. Kennedy Circle, where they would dismount and walk the rest of the way to the Embassy.

Sergeant Schuepfer, accompanied by Corporal Huss, as part of his patrol duties was checking to ensure that the rear entrance to the Norodom Compound was secure. Corporal Huss, upon moving to the nearby rear parking lot, immediately spotted a suspicious looking individual. He held his fire to be sure that the individual was not an Embassy employee. That he was not was immediately confirmed. The intruder, carrying an AK-47, walked into a lighted spot. Now, without hesitation, Corporal Huss fired his .38-caliber revolver, his only weapon, and hit the VC's lower body seriously enough to knock him down. Although apparently badly wounded, the sapper was able to crawl away and under vehicles in the parking lot. Because Corporal Huss had expended all his ammunition, he considered it unwise to attempt to capture the sapper by crawling after him.

Corporal Ryan, a member of Sergeant Bank's force, had assumed a position near the Norodom gate. He could see a jeep rapidly approaching the main gate. He recognized it as an MP patrol vehicle that had apparently been prowling the streets of Saigon. The patrol radio must have flashed the news of the enemy attack at the Embassy. With that, the two-man patrol must have sped to the Embassy to check on the situation there. The two passengers in the jeep were Sergeant Jonnie B. Thomas and Specialist Fourth Class

Owen E. Mebust. The moment the jeep stopped, Sergeant Thomas hopped out on the passenger side and turned to walk to the rear. He had barely moved when he was shot in the back by a sniper. He stumbled and then collapsed. Corporal Ryan yelled for the driver to take cover. Specialist Fourth Class Mebust must not have heard Ryan, or disregarded the warning in his eagerness to help his wounded buddy. Once out of the vehicle, he ran around it to get to Thomas. Upon reaching Thomas and realizing that he was dead, Mebust reached for his radio microphone to send a distress call but never made it, as he too was instantly killed, this time by a burst of automatic fire.

The Military Police reaction force arrived at John F. Kennedy Circle, about two blocks south of the Embassy, at 0315. Lieutenant Ribich and Sergeant Rivera had the men dismount, and the group was quickly divided into two teams. Since they were not aware of the exact situation, it was considered prudent to advance to the Embassy on foot. Within four hundred feet of the Norodom Compound the reaction force came under intense automatic fire, which forced them to take cover. However, they continued to advance. As they neared the compound, Lieutenant Ribich could not help but notice Sergeant Thomas' and Specialist Mebust's jeep, and then their bodies. There was absolutely no evidence to show how the jeep's two passengers had been killed. This was puzzling, for the sappers were inside the compound, and the two MPs died outside of it.

It was now 0337. Lieutenant Ribich, after assessing the situation, concluded that Thomas and Mebust had been mowed down by fire from outside the compound. His force continued to receive automatic fire, and Lieutenant Ribich now knew without a doubt that the fire was not only coming from the outside of the Embassy, but from a source almost directly opposite the main gate. That culprit was easily identified. It had to be the eight-story apartment building that dominated the east side of Thong Nhut and the main gate, as well. Here, unquestionably, was where the sniper and automatic fire originated. Realizing this, Lieutenant Ribich immediately ordered

Sergeant Rivera to move his fire team and to assault the building and secure it. Sergeant Rivera, even with his small force, knew that he would have to start at the top and work down. So he and his men rushed the building and continued on to the top. As they ascended the building, they found no signs of snipers or other armed individuals who obviously had quickly vacated the premises. In a minimum amount of time they reached the top of the building and moved out onto the roof, where they spotted four armed individuals. Sergeant Rivera spat out an order, and they instantly dropped their weapons. A quick examination of their identification cards surprisingly revealed that they were American civilians. They were ordered to return immediately to their rooms. It would turn out that the apartment building was the residence of a wide miscellany of individuals.

As his force cleared the building floor by floor, Rivera ordered all the residents to remain in their rooms. When his search was complete, his team secured all entrances to the building, so as to deny to the VC further entry into the building.

Thus ended a somewhat small, puzzling aspect of the Embassy battle. The mission of the twenty sappers was to get into the Embassy Compound, and to take control of it. Now it became evident that they had allies in the person of the sniper or snipers, and the shooters of the automatic weapons. One has to wonder if the sappers knew that they had allies outside. This development had to be the work of a clever planner who had looked ahead. He must have known of the apartment building and its dominance over the main entrance to the Embassy. He also must have calculated that once the attack on the Embassy commenced, men and vehicles would be drawn to the main gate on Thong Nhut, and would be lucrative targets for shooters positioned in the apartment building. So he had at least one sniper and one individual armed with an automatic weapon stashed inside the building, awaiting the commencement of the TET attack.

Now with the threat eliminated, that flank was secure. Lieutenant Ribich was also, at last, able to move his men into the

Norodom Compound. Once inside, he sought out and located Staff Sergeant Banks, who was the ranking Marine guard inside.

As events would subsequently unfold, the meeting between Lieutenant Ribich and Staff Sergeant Banks would prove to be a portentous one.

As has been mentioned, every U.S. Embassy located in the wide variety of countries around the world has assigned to it a Marine Security Guard Detachment, whose responsibility is to provide security for that Embassy. The size of those detachments varies considerably. They are based primarily on the size and importance of the country, and the political and diplomatic factors then prevailing.

Because of the uniqueness of the situation in Vietnam and Saigon, the Marine detachment was a sizeable one. It was expected that its personnel had drafted contingency plans for such things as nuisance and terrorist attacks, side-by shootings, demonstrations, and protest gatherings. The State Department planners, however, in their wildest imaginings could not have visualized or foreseen such a formidable attack on the Embassy as part of the unbelievable widespread TET offensive on the city of Saigon.

As mentioned, responsibility for the security of the Embassy rested upon the shoulders of the U.S. Marines. HAC had in Saigon and environs 450 installations for which it was responsible, but the U.S. Embassy was not one of them. The State Department assumed responsibility for their Embassy. HAC's MPs routinely patrolled the streets around it, and the MPs had a presence in the Embassy Compound, but it was limited to a two-man post. The Marines were in charge. It was their fight. However, this one was much too big for them. They could not do it alone. And so in this very grave emergency, HAC's MPs joined forces with them.

Now what was unfolding was a totally unexpected, unplanned-for contingency. The Marines and the HAC MPs certainly had never expected to be called upon to work together under such a drastic, dramatic circumstance. But there they were, operating together within the tight confines of the Embassy Compound. At night, in the dimly lit compound, they were confronting scattered, suicidal, heavily armed, diminutive individuals. The Marines and MPs would also be scattered and operating singly or in pairs. Friend and foe could easily get mixed up at such close quarters, inviting confusion and the alarming possibility of Marines and MPs firing upon one another.

Enter two individuals junior in rank who alertly, astutely, and quickly recognized that such just could not happen. The moment Lieutenant Ribich met Staff Sergeant Banks, he quickly described the deployment of Sergeant Rivera's small force. Then these two individuals made a critical decision that would have a profound impact on the entire remaining Embassy battle. They recognized that both the Marine and MP chain of command had to be kept intact, while at the same time both sides had to be completely aware of what the other was confronting. So two individuals set up an extremely simple, informal, ad hoc joint command. This makeshift action proved to be critically effective during the entire subsequent battle, and assisted greatly in bringing about the successful conclusion of the battle with no friendly fire casualties.

Following his meeting with Staff Sergeant Banks, Lieutenant Ribich contacted Sergeant Harper at the main desk to receive a report on the chancery situation. He especially had to know, and thus asked, if any sappers had gained entrance into the chancery. Sergeant Harper confirmed that none had gotten inside. With all the confusion then prevailing no one could possibly recognize or realize how critical were the words, "None have gotten inside." What those words, unbelievably, also meant was, "None will get inside. Thus, the chancery is secure."

How could that be? It could be because the sappers had an absolutely golden but fleeting window of opportunity to seize the chancery. It was theirs on a silver platter. Yes, when the sappers invaded the Embassy grounds, the chancery was theirs for the taking. There was nothing in their way. It was defenseless. Yet, they blew it!

They had just killed the only two visible military men, MPs Daniel and Sebast. The only other armed military personnel in the entire Embassy Compound at the time were Sergeant Schuepfer and

Lance Corporal Wilson, who were manning Post #12 in the Norodom Compound. This was some distance from the main door of the chancery, and was separated from it by an interior wall and locked gates. Sergeant Harper and Corporal Zahuranic were stationed at Post #1, which was in the chancery behind the main door in the lobby. Sergeant Soto was positioned on the roof of the chancery. That was the total military strength.

Included in the population of the Embassy Compound were civilians and noncombatants. At that time they consisted of the following: Mr. E. Allen Wendt, a USAID economics expert, who was serving as Embassy Night Duty Officer on the fourth floor of the chancery, two Vietnamese employees—a night watchman and a teletype operator on the ground floor—a code clerk and an Army communications operator, the CIA Night Duty Officer, and two of his men on the 4th floor.

Two others were Colonel George D. Jacobson, U.S. Army (Ret.) and Master Sergeant Robert A. Josephson, U.S. Army (Ret.), who served as associates to the ambassador. Jacobson's title was Mission Coordinator, and he lived in the French villa in the north corner of the compound behind the chancery. This was Josephson's last night in Vietnam, and he was the houseguest of Jacobson. Both were unarmed, and neither could contribute in any way to the defense of the Embassy.

As related, almost immediately after they gained entry into the Embassy grounds, sappers positioned themselves in front of the main door and quickly fired two RPGs, one after another. These splintered the main door and sent fragments into the lobby. These wounded Harper superficially and Zahuranic seriously. A tossed grenade also somehow reached the lobby.

At this point Sergeant Harper believed that it was all over. He steeled himself for the expected onslaught. With Zahuranic out of action, he was alone, but prepared to go down fighting. He knew full well from the already damaged door that two more RPGs, or four at the most, would completely shatter the door, leaving it wide open for immediate entry by a small horde of sappers, who would quickly take control of all floors of the chancery.

But amazingly, incomprehensibly, as he waited breathlessly for the next moment, which would be his last, the blow never came. No more RPGs, no sappers came slashing through his door. Moments at first, then minutes, began to pass. He continued to hear voices, and then he heard RPGs fired, but they were random shots at the upper floors. The massive, coordinated attack, much to his astonishment and huge relief, never came.

What happened? After the initial two RPGs damaged the chancery door, the sappers did the unthinkable. They did not follow up, but instead moved away. There was nothing, absolutely nothing to stop them. Incredibly, they stopped themselves. Astonishingly, it appears that after their two RPG shots, they may not have been aware of the damage they had done, and were waiting for someone to tell them what next to do. It was readily apparent that there was no someone, they were without a leader, no sergeant or lieutenant to direct, coordinate, and lead their efforts.

The only plausible explanation, but possibly the correct one, as later events would indicate, is that *the first two sappers who slipped through the blasted hole in the wall surely must have been the two team leaders.* When they died at the hands of Daniel and Sebast, the success of the operation died with them. The remaining leaderless sappers obviously did not realize that all they had to do was to join together in front of the main door of the chancery, fire a small barrage of RPGs to reduce the door to splinters, charge in and take control of the entire building. It seemed like such a simple, obvious operation. Yet, it did not happen. One of battle's rare, precious gems is surprise. This is fragile, fleeting, but also very powerful. When one has it, it must be used suddenly, quickly, without hesitation, for once its gone it can never be recalled. The sappers had surprise in the palm of their hands for a brief period, but let the unforgiving opportunity get away, squandered.

The remaining sappers without a leader were now an uncoordinated group of individuals. Without question their team leaders, during their briefing, had stressed the importance of that particular building, but the sappers were not sophisticated enough to realize the tremendous psychological impact it would have worldwide if it were in their hands. They were simple but very dedicated, capable soldiers. They knew that withdrawing from the Embassy Compound was not an option. Thus, they would fight to the finish in that relatively small box.

Although the chancery had not been captured and appeared secure, the real Embassy battle was just beginning. It would be a series of dangerous, bloody, dirty little skirmishes. The battle itself would be as "unclassic," unconventional, as one could possibly be. The "battlefield" was a tiny walled-in area with a small variety of buildings, parked cars, interior wall and gates.

The contrast between the two combatants could not be more remarkable. On one side there were the sappers, now apparently leaderless. They wore civilian attire, but were heavily armed. They were dangerous, tenacious, had been well trained on how to kill. Moreover, they were now desperate, suicidal, for they knew that they would not leave that battlefield alive. Accordingly, they would seek and destroy, take down with them as many as they possibly could.

Arriving on this battlefield after the sappers had infiltrated and deployed, were MP and Marine reaction forces. Although these elements were well aware that they would be fighting sappers, they had absolutely no idea of how many, or where they were hiding. The MPs and Marines were not nearly as heavily armed as their foe. Their mission, likewise, was seek and destroy—eliminate the sappers from the Embassy grounds.

The Embassy battle would be a series of small, isolated, uncoordinated actions—a war of attrition. Each side would seek targets of opportunity, and try to snuff them out. There would be duels between individuals.

The battle would end when the last sapper was killed or captured.

★ ★ ★

It was those individual confrontations and events that *together* brought total victory to the Embassy battle.

At this point in the battle, the sappers were in control of and roaming about the Embassy compound. The main gate had been locked early, before there was any sign of sappers. The side (vehicle) gate had been left unlocked and open until the sappers appeared and fired on Daniel and Sebast, who immediately closed and locked the gate. Thus, the only way for the sappers to gain entrance to the Embassy grounds was by crawling through the blasted hole and by scaling the ten-foot wall, both of which they did.

As for the MP and Marine reaction forces and reinforcements to come, the only options open for entry into the Embassy Compound were scaling the wall or blasting open the locked gate. Scaling the wall was briefly considered and quickly discarded. It was dark but there was visibility. Figures could be spotted. Upon reaching the top, individuals scaling the wall would be briefly silhouetted and extremely vulnerable. Gathering at the main gate to blast open the lock was also not feasible at this particular time. So the U.S. elements had used the only way readily open to them to enter the Embassy complex, which was through the Norodom Compound gate that had been opened from the inside.

Separating the sappers and the Embassy Compound from the Norodom Compound was an interior wall. For elements of the reaction forces to gain entrance into the Embassy Compound, they had to do it from the Norodom Compound, through an unlocked gate. Thus, most of the engagements in the remaining battle would take place in the rear of the chancery.

Corporal Huss and Lance Corporal Caudle had moved out into the Embassy Compound into an area near the rear parking lot. Deciding to run for the door to the generator building, Caudle received fire from automatic weapons. When he reached the generator building, Caudle rushed through the door and hit the floor as the building was being peppered. Corporal Huss was able to spot the sappers doing the firing. Since he had only a .38 revolver, which did not come close to providing him with the firepower that he needed, he returned to Staff Sergeant Banks in Norodom for more and better weapons. After Huss had left, Caudle emerged from the building only to have a sapper hiding behind a tree in the parking lot open fire at him. He jumped back inside the building, and again plopped down on the floor. It was not a bit too soon, for at the next moment a burst of fire, including an exploding rocket, hit the wall.

Corporal Huss provided Lieutenant Ribich and Staff Sergeant Banks with a quick, brief situation report. Banks immediately headed out with Sergeant Jimerson, Sergeant Spersrud, Corporal Marshall and two MPs for the generator building. Two minutes after Staff Sergeant Banks had departed at about 0400, an MP patrol, which had responded to an Embassy distress call, reported to Lieutenant Ribich. This patrol was equipped with an M-60 machine gun. Since the MPs and Marines were seriously outgunned by the sappers, Lieutenant Ribich instructed the MPs to follow him. They moved out at a dead run around the Office of the Special Assistant (OSA) building to the generator building. Ribich immediately placed the machine gun in the doorway and began firing at suspected locations of sappers among vehicles in the parking lot. Ribich returned to the Norodom Compound, leaving Banks in charge.

Sergeant Jimerson kept darting outside to try to draw fire and provide targets for the M-60 machine gun. Lance Corporal Caudle, who had been the first one in the building, was now absorbed into the team.

Staff Sergeant Banks decided to move his team, one at a time, through the open doorway into the parking lot. Sergeant Jimerson—who was armed with a Beretta, which gave him more and better fire power than a pistol—jumped out first, so as to be able to lay down a base of fire for the others. As he stepped through the doorway, he spotted two sappers running across the parking lot and fired all twenty of his rounds, knocking down both of them.

As he turned back to the doorway, he was the target of a great burst of fire and a rocket, which exploded close to the door and to him. He received a small wound to his left hand. Still a bit dazed by the concussion, the continuing fire found him again. He received a second wound to his right leg. It was now perfectly obvious to Staff Sergeant Banks that they were badly outgunned by the sappers, who had selected good positions and were now entrenched in the parking lot. A further advance or attack was out of the question. So he decided to withdraw temporarily to the front of the Norodom Compound with part of his force. He would leave two military policemen with the M-60 machine gun and two members of the team to hold their position and cover the area.

While the two MPs were administering first aid to him and preparing him for movement, Sergeant Jimerson shouted that a rocket was coming in, and immediately the two MPs jumped on him to cover his body. The rocket exploded, spraying the area with shrapnel and wounding one of the MPs in his left arm. The protection provided by the flak jackets worn by the MPs prevented Jimerson from being wounded again. There is no question that Jimerson showed great daring and courage and certainly distinguished himself during this brief engagement with the sappers.

At about this time Corporal Marshall and Corporal Ryan, inside the Norodom Compound, climbed to the top of the OSA Building, which afforded them an excellent field of fire into the Embassy Compound. Ryan followed Marshall as they climbed up. Not long after he positioned himself, Marshall noticed that fire from the M-60 seemed to be forcing sappers to leave their positions and move about. Corporal Ryan, armed with a Beretta and about two hundred rounds of ammunition, suddenly noticed that three sappers had moved into range in front of their position. He immediately opened fire. The sappers instantly realized that they had moved too far, and that men on the roof were firing at them. Without hesitation they stopped, turned, and raced toward the safety of the main entrance. Corporal Ryan, aiming at the fleeing sappers, fired another burst, and amazingly all three sappers went down. Then Marshall observed a sapper crawling from behind a planter near the chancery, fired several rounds at him, and apparently killed him.

Although two more sappers were spotted, before they could fire on them, Corporal Ryan himself was wounded in the head, left arm, and left leg by a rocket that hit the OSA Building. Wounded in the face by shrapnel from that round, Corporal Ryan was assisted down from the roof by Corporal Marshall, and handed over to several Military Policemen on the ground. Marshall returned to his position on the roof with Ryan's Beretta and about one hundred rounds of ammunition. Ryan was moved close to the front, and he requested that an MP put a field dressing over his wound. Fearing that a piece of shrapnel protruding from his head might kill him if moved, Lieutenant Ribich instructed them to leave the wound alone. As Ryan was evacuated, Corporal Wilson climbed up to the roof to assist Marshall.

About this time, Staff Sergeant Banks, using the phone in the guard shack, contacted Sergeant Harper in the chancery lobby. He was vastly relieved to learn that Sergeant Harper and the chancery main door had not been assaulted in any way since their initial confrontation. Harper declared that he was well aware of sapper movements on the Embassy grounds, but, amazingly, they had left him alone. Banks then explained to Harper that a decision had been made to wait until daybreak for the big assault on the Embassy Compound, and assured Harper that they would get to him at the earliest opportunity.

About 0418 the Military Police desk received a request from Lieutenant Ribich for a substantial and varied supply of additional ammunition. Lieutenant Colonel George contacted Sergeant Kuldas, who was his traffic chief, and gave him the important mission. Sergeant Kuldas without hesitation departed for the ammunition bunker, dug out the various types that were needed, and in no time personally delivered the shipment to the Embassy.

Captain James T. Chester, Commander of B Company, 716th Military Police Battalion, departed from the International Hotel at 0430 with a fifty-man reaction force. After arriving within one block of the Embassy, Captain Chester, along with Lieutenant Ribich, who had joined him, Sergeant First Class Williams, and two Military Policemen, moved on to the Norodom Compound.

Fire from that compound into the Embassy Compound seemed

to be effective in pinning down the sappers. Nevertheless, Captain Chester and Lieutenant Ribich wanted to be sure that all avenues of escape were closed to the sappers, and that they would remain trapped in the embassy compound. Accordingly, they decided at about 0500 to position Chester's force along the street in front of the chancery.

Meanwhile, Corporal Marshall and Corporal Wilson, who had been positioned for some time on top of the OSA Building, spotted a sapper behind a tree and fired in his direction. The sapper returned fire, hitting Corporal James C. Marshall in the neck. He fell to the roof. Corporal Wilson rushed to his aid and found that the shot had killed Marshall. The fire toward the roof now became heavy. Apparently the sappers had discovered that was where much of their grief had come from. With that, Wilson yelled to the MPs to get off the roof.

At that hot bed of activity, the generator building, action continued. Three Marine reinforcements, Sergeants David R. Bothwell, Richard L. Johnson, and Joseph S. Wolff, left the Marine House, scaled a back shed, and joined Sergeant Reed, who was already in the area. The three of them quickly moved to the rear of the generator building. The moment that they were settled, they began pouring a steady volume of fire at the sappers who had taken cover behind cars in the parking lot. Sergeant Bothwell spotted and killed two sappers who were at the far corner of the chancery building. In retaliation, sappers behind a pillar near the chancery began firing at the team on top of the generator building. As the sappers moved to better firing positions, Sergeant Johnson opened fire with his Beretta, forcing them to move for cover, which provided an opportunity for Sergeant Reed to kill a member of the group. The remaining two sappers, now without cover, stopped and began firing again and so did Sergeant Johnson. One of his bursts hit the leading sapper, who went down but managed to get back up, and both rushed around to the shelter afforded them on the opposite side of the building. The team had been firing furiously and now found themselves short of ammunition. This was a good time for one of its members, Sergeant Wolff, to undertake the risky but necessary trip back to the Norodom Compound for a quick re-supply.

In the Norodom Compound, Lieutenant Ribich was in contact with the Military Police radio net control station, WACO, and was told that Lieutenant Colonel George had declared that it was now time for the assault on the Embassy Compound and the elimination of the remaining sappers. Ribich gave the order to move out at 0700, which would be daylight. Shortly after, he was told to move his kickoff fifteen minutes earlier, to 0645. Once the order "Go!" was given, the Embassy battle would soon come to a close.

The battle had not by any means followed a predictable pattern. It had been weird, no continuity, no common thread of any kind through it, and with totally unexpected twists and turns. The sappers had roamed the grounds firing away at anything they saw moving. The Marines and MPs did their best to pick off the sappers one by one.

Both sides were formidable adversaries. The sappers were predictably fanatical, resourceful, and had used the great firepower of their AK-47s to full advantage. For a small band, their ferocious fight had a great impact.

The Marines and MPs, likewise, had acquitted themselves superbly. They were considerably under-gunned, but were tenacious and successful in picking off sappers.

But now, with the assault about to kick off, it would finally be over for the sappers still remaining. They had weathered an intense, demanding, stressful and costly night. And at this point they had just about "shot their wad." Now they were facing a force that would outnumber and simply overpower them. However, they would still have a couple of surprises up their sleeves. Like pesky varmints, there was still "no quit" in them, and they would continue to lead a surprisingly merry chase until they went down fighting.

From the outset of their attack on the Embassy, it had been expected that the chancery would be the focal point, the centerpiece, of the Embassy battle, and it would be where the battle would begin and where it would end. Amazingly, after two RPG shots and a tossed grenade at the main entrance, the chancery would "never be heard from again." The Embassy battle would end in the most unlikely place, in the most unlikely way. The final minutes would be almost unbelievable.

The moment the word "Go!" was sent out, Specialist Fourth Class Healey and Sergeant Shook drove a jeep right to the main gate and shot the lock off, but much to their surprise and chagrin they could not force the gate open. Big, burly Sergeant Kuldas and several MPs added weight to the vehicle, and pushed it against the gate. The best that they could do was to force it open enough to allow the members of the attacking force to enter the compound one at a time.

Healey was the first man through. After him, the following troops fanned out like a wide sweeper across the grounds, with their weapons at the ready and with their safeties off. The first sapper reaction was almost instantaneous. As Healey was moving along in front of the door to the chancery, he detected a movement to his left, turned and watched in horror as a sapper tossed a grenade at him, which landed at his feet. Healey instantly shot and killed him. But seconds had elapsed, and Healey steeled himself for the grenade that was ready to explode at the very next second and probably kill him. Much to his great surprise and astonishing reprieve, the grenade at his feet was a dud. He had been spared.

While some of the Military Policemen were moving along the wall and across the compound, engaging the sappers in the front part of the compound, Sergeant Rivera's force of military policemen, along with Marines, entered the parking lot from the Norodom Compound. As they were moving along the parking lot, Sergeant Kuldas, Corporal Moyer, and Specialist Fourth Class Singer noticed bloodstains on the Embassy Compound side of the wall that separated it from the Norodom Compound. Footprints on the wall indicated that it was highly likely that a sapper had scaled the wall. Kuldas and Singer moved back into the Norodom Compound, and proceeded to move along the walkway that separated it from the OSA Building and the wall. They continued to follow the bloody tracks and came upon the dog run, where they surprisingly spotted an abandoned AK-47 and more blood in the middle of the run. It appeared incongruous, but the sapper seemed to have been attacked by a dog. In a sudden state of panic, he must have dropped his gun and made a run for the safety of the OSA Building. Sure enough, Sergeant Kuldas found bloodstains at a doorway to the office building. He entered the building and found a blood trail on the hallway floor, which he followed to the door of the map room, which he found was locked from the inside. With that he shouted for someone inside to open the door. With no response forthcoming, he blasted the door. As the door flew open, there stood the someone, a frightened, shaking, unarmed sapper with his hands straight up in surrender.

This turned out to be quite a story. Some days after the end of the Embassy battle, the February 9, 1968 issue of *Life Magazine* carried a full front page picture showing a sapper with a bloodstained face, two very bloody arms, and a shirt covered with blood, his arms stiffly straight up in surrender. He is standing between the powerfully built Sergeant Kuldas, who towers above him, and a younger, robust, tough-looking MP. By contrast what is seen is a tiny, youthful, bewildered, innocent appearing individual, but until captured, he was a potent, lethal, dangerous weapon. Of the twenty sappers, nineteen were killed, and this was the only one wounded and captured. He was not able to go down fighting like his compatriots, because he had abandoned his AK-47.

Shortly after moving through the steel door separating the Norodom Compound from the parking area, Sergeant Rivera immediately spotted three sappers, took them under fire, and it appeared that he had quickly killed the three. After that, he and his team continued to sweep the parking lot area to ensure that if there were any sappers left there, they were all dead.

Then followed another absolutely bizarre confrontation. It would be an almost hour-long shootout with, of all things, a single, wounded sapper. This was not an ordinary guy. He was frantic, fanatical, an amazingly tenacious, clever, diehard sapper, who turned out to be a one-man army. He provided one more surprising twist in the already utterly strange Embassy battle. No! The final shot would not be fired, the last sapper killed, at or in the chancery. It was in, of all places, the mission coordinator's quarters in the northeast corner of the Embassy Compound. As Sergeant Rivera, with his Military Policemen and Marines, moved along the Embassy wall, word reached them that a wounded sapper, seeking refuge, had just burst into the mission coordinator's quarters.

This was a two-story, white stucco villa. A very uneasy and greatly troubled Colonel Jacobson had spent the night in the upstairs hall of that building. It must have been a frightening night for him to hear firing all around him, not knowing if it was friend or foe, not knowing what was really happening. Worst of all, he had expected sappers to burst into his home at any moment, and he was unarmed and defenseless. He had found a hand grenade in the desk in his bedroom, which he had been clutching. If sappers had come charging up the stairs at him, the one grenade was his only weapon.

Sometime after daylight, he moved from the back hall to the top of the stairs. As he looked down the steps, he was astonished to note bloody spots on the rug at the bottom of the steps. Colonel Jacobson instantly knew that he had company in the villa. Fright began edging toward panic. He still had phone contact outside of the villa and he recognized that if there ever was a time to use it, it was now. He sent out an emergency call about his dangerous predicament. The "word" soon after, somehow reached Sergeant Rivera. Without hesitation he moved his force right to the villa.

The first effort by the Military Policemen and Marines upon reaching the building was to rush the back door. They were met by a hail of fire from the very alert, dangerous sapper, who drove them back with his powerful AK-47. Sergeant Rivera, without hesitation, slipped his force toward the front door. Once again it was Healey who grabbed the lead, kicked open a door on the front porch and, along with Marine Sergeant Bothwell, charged inside. Someone was waiting, for Sergeant Bothwell immediately received a shot in his thigh. Under fire, Healey quickly dragged the Marine out of the house and onto the porch, and then threw a grenade into the villa. It was not immediately known if the grenade had any effect on the sapper, but the explosion stunned Colonel Jacobson as he lay on the top step ready to use his one grenade if the sapper climbed the stairs to him.

Captain O'Brien now appeared on the scene and went right to the aid of Bothwell, his wounded Marine. He charged up the porch steps, and started to pull Bothwell to safety, when of all things, a grenade came at them from out of the house. O'Brien reacted instantly and covered his sergeant, only to be wounded himself. It was obvious to all that the sapper, like a cornered rat, was fighting a desperate and clever battle. The situation and the evacuation of Bothwell became even more complicated. While all this was taking place, two teargas grenades were pushed through the bars of a first floor window by MPs. O'Brien quickly slipped a gas mask over Bothwell's face and then over his own. Healey, nearby without a gas mask, clearly felt its early sting.

The very desperate Colonel Jacobson appeared at his bedroom window shouting frantically for a weapon. He was certain that the CS had now swept through the first floor, and would force the sapper upstairs. Once again it was Healey. He stood completely vulnerable on the lawn close to the building, and tossed up to Jacobson a .45 pistol and a gas mask. Once he had them in hand, Colonel Jacobson did not waste a moment getting his gas mask on and selecting a corner defensive position. Now he was a bit more ready for the next development, whatever that might be. The tables had suddenly turned in his favor.

The sapper, without a gas mask, was probably half blind. Going up the stairs now dominated by Colonel Jacobson was the only way to get away from the gas. So as he began his ascent, he also began to fire his AK-47. He climbed the steps as quickly as he could, and fired his powerful weapon back and forth up the stairs. On a much broader scale this might be termed, "reconnaissance by fire." Some of his shots were hitting just over Jacobson's head. Just as he was about to reach the top, he shifted his position a bit. With that, Colonel

Jacobson jumped up and fired twice at point blank range. The sapper never had a chance, and that small, amazing, one-man fighting machine was instantly killed. As he began to tumble down the stairs, Colonel Jacobson grasped his AK-47. Now he believed that he was much better prepared to greet the sappers who were sure to follow.

However, the movement that he now heard at the bottom of the steps was not more sappers. No, it was Military Policemen. Believing that the sapper was still covering the front door, they smashed open the rear door. The last sapper was dead.

This totally unexpected, incongruous, unbelievable climax to the Embassy fight had ended. The Embassy battle was over.

Observations

It is my firm belief that Specialist Fourth Class Charles L. Daniel and Private First Class William E. Sebast, although never so recognized, remain the great but *unsung* heroes of the Embassy battle.

As events unfolded and the fight evolved, the enemy attackers became a group of *rudderless* sappers. It is almost a certainty that the first two sappers through the Embassy wall were the "brains," the leaders of that small group. Had they not been mowed down at the very outset of the battle by Daniel and Sebast, it would have been only moments later that the chancery would have been assaulted and quickly occupied on all floors by the sappers. This did not happen. Daniel and Sebast saved the chancery. Even more importantly, they saved American lives. With a dozen or more sappers, each with an AK-47, holed up and holding on in the chancery, it would have been an absolute major undertaking to regain control of and to clear the chancery. The assault would have been murderous and extremely costly. Entering the tight confines of the building, climbing up the stairs in the face of heavy fire coming down the stairs, could have been total disaster. Bringing in troops by helicopter would not have helped, for the roof and helipad were easily closed off.

To the vast relief of a multitude, the unthinkable never happened. Daniel and Sebast gave up their lives, but saved the day.

Daniel and Sebast: genuine heroes in the Embassy battle.

Contrary to newspaper, magazine, television accounts, and assertions by individuals, and as here already described:

The VC *never:*

Seized the chancery.

Held the chancery.

Captured the chancery.

Entered the chancery.

★ ★ ★

The MP log had this entry:

0420 General Westmoreland calls, orders first priority effort to recapture the U.S. Embassy.

At 0420 the MPs and Marines had total control of the Norodom Compound, had fought and killed sappers in the back part of the Embassy Compound, and held control of the chancery. All that was left to secure was a portion at the ground of the front part of the Embassy Compound. At that very moment Captain Chester was departing for the Embassy with his fifty- man reaction force to help do just that.

★ ★ ★

Another genuine hero: He was merely a private first class, but Paul V. Healey, during the Embassy Battle, was always in the forefront, the first man out. He demonstrated great initiative, determination, courage, and selflessness. For his actions in the fight he was awarded the Distinguished Service Cross (DSC) for extraordinary heroism.

★ ★ ★

Some months after the TET Offensive, there were still scars on the chancery façade and in its lobby. But there was also something new in that lobby. There had been a plaque erected commemorating the U.S. military men who died defending the Embassy. The words on the plaque read: I*n memory of the brave men who died January 31, 1968, defending this Embassy against the Viet Cong: Sp4 Charles L. Daniel, MPC; Cpl. James C. Marshall, USMC; Sp4 Owen E. Mebust, MPC; Pfc. William E. Sebast, MPC; Sergeant Jonnie B. Thomas, MPC.*

★ ★ ★

Except for the last hour and a half, the Embassy Battle was fought at night with but dim light. For good reason, the main outdoor Embassy lights had never been turned on.

The Embassy fight ended at 0830. The Embassy was officially declared secure at 0915.

During the Embassy Battle five Americans (four MPs and one Marine) were killed and fifteen were wounded.

The moment the fight was over at the Embassy, the military policemen returned to their headquarters to react and respond to the endless demands for their assistance and support in fighting off the VC in various parts of Saigon.

★ ★ ★

A Great Irony: In 1975, seven years later, the last Americans evacuated from Vietnam and Saigon took off in helicopters from the helipad on the roof of the chancery of the American Embassy in Saigon. That was the Embassy where personnel of Headquarters Area Command (HAC) fought gallantly and courageously, and were wounded and died, to save it from a vicious Communist assault during an earlier era.

In 1975, almost immediately after the last helicopter had left the roof, the Communists seized, captured, held, and entered the chancery and the Embassy Compound. In essence, our government ceded the U.S. Embassy in Saigon to the Communists.

For us who had diligently and courageously tried to protect it, it was a troubling, disheartening, sobering page in our nation's history.

Damaged front of the chancery.

RPG hits seal at the main door.

19 dead, this sapper was the only survivor.

Hole blown in the wall by the sappers at the very outset of the battle.

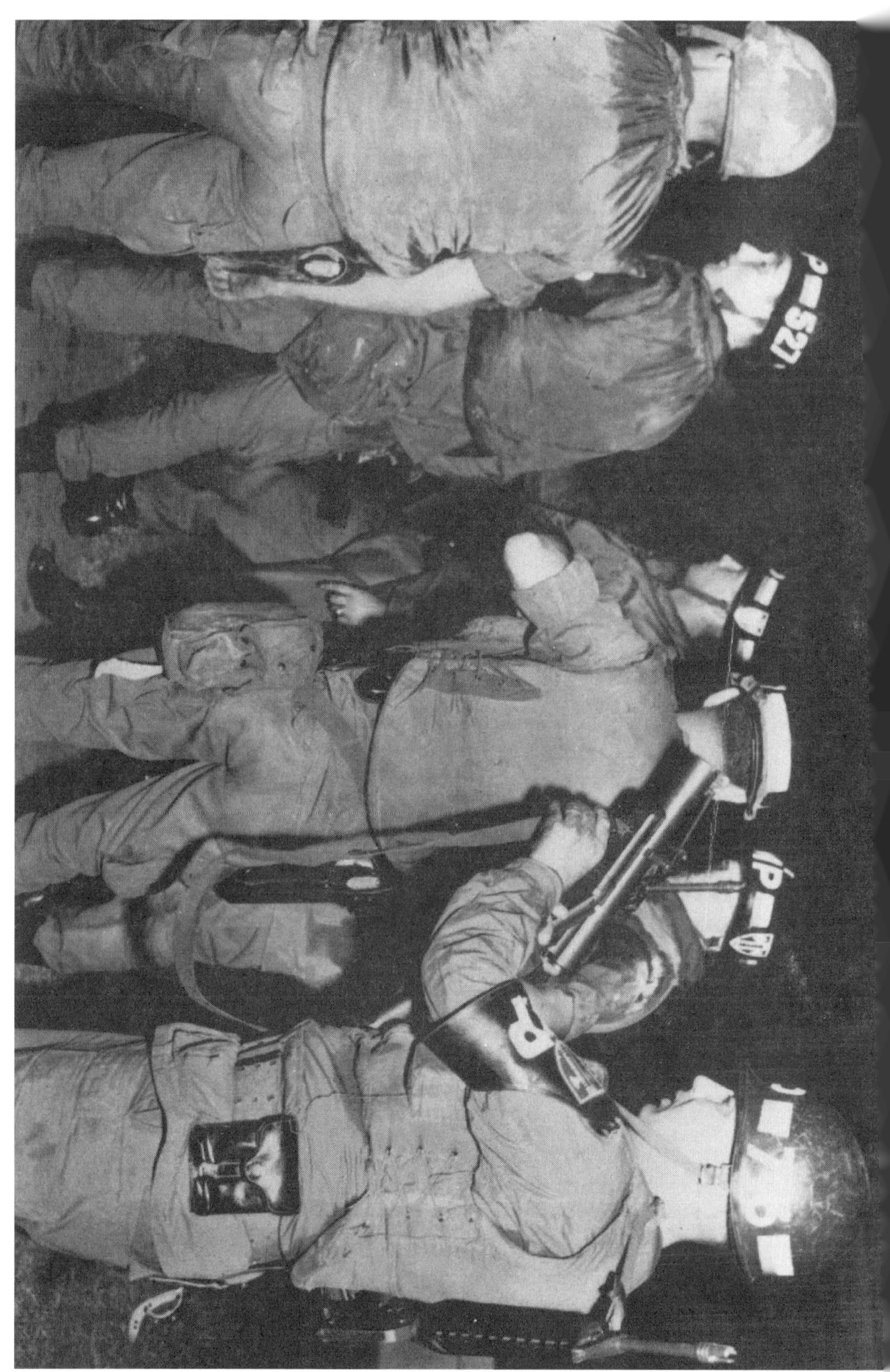

Early arrivals at the Embassy.

At the base of the chancery.

Entering Norodom Gate.

Poised and ready.

It's over. Ready to move on to the next job.

The end came on Embassy grounds.

Death came near the Embassy planters.

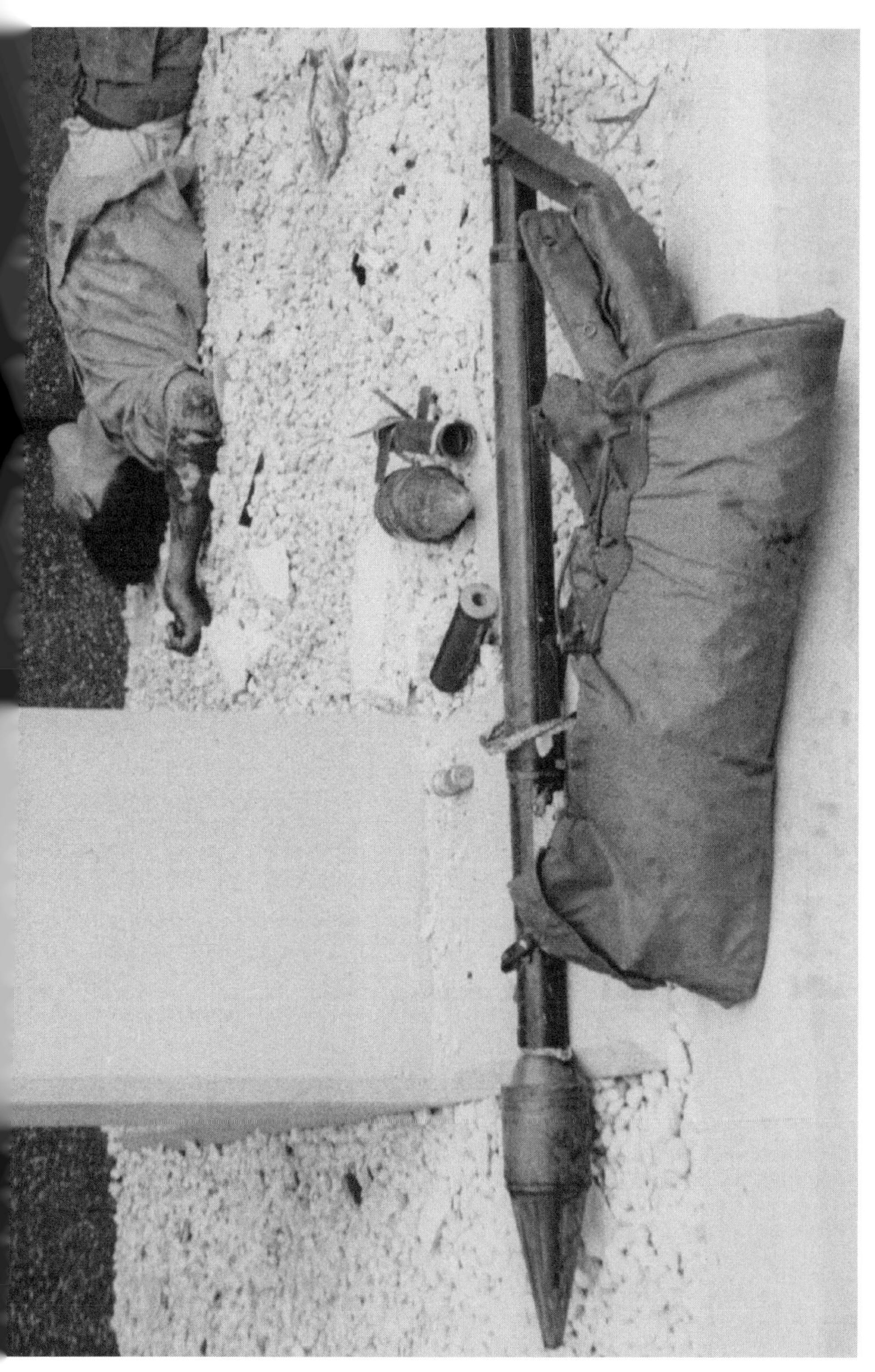

Never got to shoot it.

Three at one time.

Random RPG shots at chancery facade.

Rockets never fired.

He tried.

PITCHED BATTLES AND ENGAGEMENTS

CHAPTER 9
BOQ #3 BATTLE

The BOQ (Bachelor Officers' Quarters) #3 fight was an especially intense, vicious, violent, pitched battle. That engagement was by far the most costly in casualties suffered by the MPs and HAC personnel during the entire Saigon Battle.

Yet, there is here a great irony. Although it will always be known as the fight for BOQ #3, that building was never assaulted or attacked. No, the target for the VC was the Vietnamese Joint General Staff (JGS) Compound nearby. For the attacking Communists, the JGS was the second most important Vietnamese complex, after the Presidential Palace in Saigon. It was one of the "Big Five" to be discussed. Whereas the Communists made some drastic miscalculations and badly botched their most unsuccessful attempt to seize the Presidential Palace, they had a better plan and were better organized to take control of the JGS. However, even here they were quickly thrown off stride.

The attack on the JGS Compound, a kilometer or so east of Tan Son Nhut, began at about 0300. There was immediate confusion at the main gate. The sappers were initially delayed because they had difficulty forcing the gate open, but under cover of supporting fire from a nearby pagoda, they were able to wrench it open. Just as they were about to charge into the compound, apparently out of nowhere, an MP jeep appeared. This surprised and distracted them. (Later, captured VC would claim that everywhere they turned, they would come face to face with MPs. This was a classic example.) The sappers, of course, stopped, turned and directed their fire at the MPs. Almost immediately, two more MP jeeps appeared and joined the one that had disturbed the attack. The first jeep was already sending an urgent message reporting that he was receiving fire at BOQ #3, and needed assistance at once. BOQ #3 was a lucrative target. Everyone in Saigon, including the MP, knew that it was the residence of colonels and junior generals who worked at MACV. The Provost Marshal's office, which received the message, understandably believed that it was the BOQ that was under attack. There was no time for delay, so the 716th MP Company located nearby at Tan Son Nhut was tasked to send at once a reaction force to BOQ #3. The MPs at BOQ #3 had taken cover behind their jeeps parked by the front gate of the BOQ, but were still firing at and receiving fire from the sappers who obviously were trying to suppress the MPs who had interrupted and interfered with their initial attack.

So the VC were not the least bit interested in BOQ #3. It was still the JGS Compound that they were after. More sappers showed themselves, and they blew open the north gate with RPGs. Now behind the sappers came members of what would turn out to be a battalion of VC. They immediately seized a building inside the compound that they believed to be the critically important JGS headquarters. Alas, what they seized was, instead, merely the headquarters of a support company. Nevertheless, it took the ARVN forces the rest of the day to round up the VC elements inside the compound.

That battle would pale by comparison with the bloody, difficult fight that also took place all day, not much more than a block away.

The reaction force that the MPs at BOQ #3 had requested had mounted up in a minimum amount of time, and they were soon on the way. The element was commanded by Lieutenant Waltman of Company C, 716th MP Battalion, which was stationed at Tan Son Nhut. It was still the middle of the night, so the force departed from the air base under blackout conditions. This particular force consisted of a lead jeep with the windshield down, occupied by Lieutenant Waltman and his driver, Specialist Four John R. Van Wagner. The vehicle was followed by a two-and-a-half ton, six-by-six truck that was jammed with military policemen. There were three MPs in the cab and seventeen more in the bed of the truck. These men sat facing one another on two parallel benches that folded up. A three-man gun jeep followed closely behind. All men were in their combat gear, wearing steel helmets with large MP letters on the front and flak jackets.

Since they were stationed at the air base, they were very familiar with that part of the city. They well knew that there was a street that would take them directly from a gate at Tan Son Nhut almost to the front gate of BOQ #3. However, it was a main artery, was broad and well traveled. That certainly was the quickest, most direct way in. Since it was also the most obvious, Waltman felt uneasy and leery about using it, and decided that a more indirect route would not take much longer and would surely be safer. So he turned into an inconspicuous, dark, narrow, unnamed alley that would take him to a side gate near the JGS Compound, quite close to BOQ #3.

After turning into the alley, the small convoy moved along it slowly, carefully, and quietly. Lieutenant Waltman's jeep was nearing the end of the alley, and he stopped it so that he could pull the vehicle over and proceed the rest of the way on foot. The troop truck also slowed, as did the gun jeep behind it.

Suddenly, without warning, out of nowhere—*horror, disaster, tragedy*! In but an instant, with one blow, twenty military policemen were either dead or very severely wounded, and the truck that had carried them was totally destroyed. For just a brief moment, as though time was frozen, the alley was deathly still. Then screams from the painfully wounded pierced the night air. Then from the entrenched VC came murderous fire spewing forth upon the truck and the area all around it.

What in the world had happened? Apparently, a company-sized VC unit that appeared to be a part of the force whose mission it was to attack the JGS Compound had entered the alley just a short time before the Military Policemen. They immediately climbed up, seized, and moved into the top floors of the buildings lining the alley, and took cover behind the shoulder-high walls that ran almost the length of the alley. The VC understandably wanted to be as inconspicuous as possible, but very alert, as they assembled and prepared for their final advance on the JGS Compound. They surely never expected fighting elements to close in on the alley, right on their heels. However, they reacted instantly, and well knew that they had destroyed a truck, causing extensive casualties. What they did not know was what else might be crowding in and closing around them. Since they occupied the most advantageous positions, they must have decided to delay their advance on the JGS, to stay put, and be ready for what else might happen

Where did they come from? Why did they choose, of all places, that dark, narrow alley? One can only offer conjecture. It seems uncanny, but they must have followed the same thought process that Lieutenant Waltman had. They were the aggressors, the attackers, the intruders, the infiltrators, operating in a totally new environment. They wanted to slither in quietly, almost invisibly, if possible. This required them to use the most inconspicuous route of which they were aware, which turned out to be the alley.

In combat we continually attempt to guess what the enemy is thinking and planning, what his intentions are, so that we are prepared to outfox him when he commits himself. What we sometimes forget is that the enemy, in a similar manner, is also trying to read our minds and guess our actions. The result, as so often happens—a meeting engagement. It happened again, this time in the alley—boom—face to face, head to head.

Specialist Four Van Wagner, the driver of the lead jeep with Lieutenant Waltman still aboard, responded immediately to the attack by gunning his jeep right out of the alley, and bringing it to a stop near BOQ #3. At the first shots, the gun jeep in the rear backed furiously all the way out of the alley, completely untouched. The big, powerful, deadly, unforgiving blow was directed at the large, lucrative, obvious target, the truck transporting the military policemen. It never had a chance. The VC fired their deadly RPGs at a range of only ten feet (they had protection from the walls). Simultaneously, they set off loud explosives that lit up the alley with bright flashes. The concussions from these were so powerful that they blew the tires off the rims of the wheels, and crushed almost flat some of the steel pots that had been on the heads of the military policemen. The enemy continued to "pile on" by saturating the area with fire from their automatic weapons. As earlier mentioned, all twenty of the men were instant casualties. They had all been hit, many in several places. Some died instantly, others subsequently died from their multiple wounds. Sixteen of the twenty did not survive.

The loss of so many men so quickly, of course, resulted in immediate and continued soul searching. The 716th MP Battalion's standard operating procedure specified that when called to a confrontation the MPs would not boldly drive to it, but would dismount some distance from it, and go the rest of the way on foot. This situation required split second decisions. The alley alone was about two hundred meters long. That was more than a long block away from BOQ #3. The call from that installation indicated an emergency. It was known that BOQ #3 was guarded by a single MP in a kiosk in front of the building. He had been reinforced by three MP jeeps, with a total of six more military policemen. This was hardly a potent force to resist an assault on BOQ #3, which to them appeared to be developing. The reaction force understandably assumed that they were confronted with an urgent situation, and for them it was boldness or caution, and it was boldness that won out.

There was no way of knowing, and who would have expected, that the VC would move in so quickly, and entrench themselves so cleverly, in that obscure alley. There is room for further conjecture. If the MPs had dismounted in a safe area, and moved single file up the alley, they could have been picked off one at a time or mowed down like ten pins, before they could exit from the alley.

It was dark, the VC were there first, they had picked their spots. They certainly did not plan it that way, but they lucked out. They came up with the perfect ambush. The military policemen never stood a chance, and for them it was a no-win situation. In this case it was the VC who held the four aces.

At BOQ #3, there was a considerable amount of firing all

around the installation. Fire was still being directed toward the MPs, and there were rounds hitting nearby that were directed at or were spewing out of the JGS Compound, a French villa set back from the street. Yet, BOQ #3 was never directly attacked or assaulted. During the early firing, several officer occupants, fearing that it was being attacked, rushed out the door, led by Brigadier General Earl Cole with pistol in hand, to see if they could help. However, because of their rank and vulnerability, Lieutenant Waltman, just in from the alley, forced them back inside their billet.

Discounting the trailing gun jeep, which was never in the action, Lieutenant Waltman and Specialist Four Van Wagner were the only ones from the reaction force to have escaped unscathed.

Understandably, there was for them a tremendous sense of urgency. Despite the firing and confusion around BOQ #3, Waltman rushed to the kiosk, grabbed the guard's radio inside, and reported in detail of what had happened in the alley. He was obviously in an agitated state, and his excited words spewed forth. He made it clearly known that there were dead MPs who needed to be removed, seriously wounded MPs who required immediate evacuation, and a heavily armed and defended alley to be cleared. So he pleaded that a follow up reaction force be dispatched without delay.

Knowing that it would take time for reinforcements to arrive, Waltman and Van Wagner just could not sit and wait for them. They were like two men possessed. They had to do something. So they returned to the alley resolved to make a mighty effort to reach the blown-up truck.

★ ★ ★

From the moment that I reached my headquarters after speeding away from my residence, and sank into my desk chair, the receiver of my telephone had hardly left my ear. I was monitoring a myriad of separate, critical confrontations, and trying to respond appropriately to the wide variety of requests and demands that were reaching my desk. I was particularly concerned about and paying close attention to the early reports reaching me about the attack on the U.S. Embassy. Every now and then the receiver would leave my ear, as a member of my staff interrupted me, and brought information or asked of me something that was more important than what I was hearing over the phone. I looked up and knew that such was the case as my operations officer entered my office and approached my desk. Intuitively, I knew that this was very bad news. His face was ashen, and his eyes seemed out of focus. Without preliminaries, this usually composed individual blurted out in detail the astonishing and most shocking news about the destroyed truck and heavy personnel casualties. My chin dropped like a ten-pound weight. I had already been hearing much disquieting and disturbing news from "out there," but I was stunned and stricken by this new, unbelievably tragic news. I was totally unprepared to receive such a blow so huge, and to have it come so soon.

I laid the receiver down on my desk, and waved out my staff officer. I had to gather myself; I had to have a moment to think. I instantly recognized how devastating this was to the Military Policemen; I knew that they had been rocked back on their heels, and that it would take a brief period for them to gather themselves. What particularly alarmed me was the effect it would have on Military Police resources. They had lost a reaction force and now a second would be on the way. This was a big hunk of people taken out of the strength of an MP company to be involved so early and deeply in one engagement, in one location with a long fight still to be played out. Yet, we just could not abandon the alley. I concluded that it was vital and urgent to get some fresh troops into the alley as soon as possible, troops that would *augment* the military policemen.

I called back my operations officer and instructed him to commit HAC's Quick Reaction Force #1 (QRF #1) at once. They were to move into the alley with a simple, mission-type order—to pick up the pieces, to take whatever action the existing situation required, and to work closely and with good coordination with the military police elements that were being deployed.

QRF #1 was commanded by Captain Drolla. It was a force of about thirty-five men assigned to HAC. Those individuals were my "cooks, bakers, and candlestick makers." Not one of them had ever had tactical training. They were support personnel. The thirty-five men had never—not a single time—gathered together. They did not know one another, except for some in passing. They were anything but a team. They had never before worn steel helmets and flak jackets. They had never been issued live ammunition for the purpose of killing people. That is the force that I sent into that alley.

★ ★ ★

Not knowing when reinforcements would arrive at the alley, Waltman and Van Wagner endeavored mightily to reach the demolished truck. They used their jeep and palm trees that lined the alley as cover, but as they edged closer toward the truck, their actions were detected and fire burst forth from weapons up in the buildings overlooking the alley, and was far too heavy for them to try to continue to advance. For these two dedicated and courageous individuals it was pure agony, totally frustrating and demoralizing, to hear the painful, plaintive cries of desperation coming from the seriously wounded in and around the truck.

Then, surprisingly and seemingly out of nowhere, appeared three wounded MPs. They had somehow hunched low, wiggled, and crawled out of the alley to safety. Waltman soon had them at BOQ #3, where they waited for an ambulance to get through.

For a brief period, Van Wagner became a kind of lone ranger. He fought a single-handed battle to get to the wounded. He somehow made it to a roof overlooking the alley and fired what he hoped would be suppressive fires. He ran back down to the alley prepared to move closer, only to receive fire again. He repeated this effort, but again to no avail. The VC were dug in and alert for any movement, and he was stuck. Waltman and Van Wagner had given it their absolutely best shot, and were now forced to give up their two-man crusade.

They dreaded knowing that all they could do was to sit and wait. They had been so deeply and intensely involved in the alley battle that they could easily have concluded that their battle was the only fight in town. However, while Waltman was in the kiosk sending out his alley report, he overheard on the WACO MP net much excited and frantic traffic about other engagements taking place all over town, and particularly the Embassy Battle. And from his position at BOQ #3 he could see flares over the Tan Son Nhut Air Base and hear sounds of battle emanating from that location. It was disheartening for him to recognize that under those circumstances, it did not bode well for him to be receiving the reinforcements that he had requested any time soon. So, for him and Van Wagner a forced wait would be almost unbearable.

But much to his great surprise and excitement, no sooner had those thoughts crossed his mind than an electrifying message reached him: the second reaction force, led by Lieutenant Joseph Cisneros, was only a block away from the alley. Cisneros soon informed Waltman that he had been able to close up, and had moved most of his force into position at the mouth and left side of the alley. Waltman immediately warned Cisneros not to look for VC at ground level, but to expect a reaction from upper floors and roofs of buildings.

Cisneros quickly committed a small force to get a "feel" of the situation and the enemy they were facing. The squad moved into the alley, and immediately got a very strong taste of what was out there lurking in wait for them. As though Cisneros had touched a button, down came heavy, reverberating fire directed at his troops. The VC blew up a Claymore and threw out much small arms and automatic fire. Trying to advance under those circumstances would be very difficult, but the effort had to continue. Cisneros moved a machine gun team and four MPs into what he considered a good firing position on the roof of a building next to him. The crew fired at VC positions in buildings opposite them, heavily splattering them, but the enemy was well dug in and it did no good. As though in answer, the VC tossed out grenades that wounded the first of Cisneros' MPs.

HAC QRF #1 had been poised, primed, and ready to respond to a call when it came. That call came very much sooner than expected. They pushed out with little delay to the aid of the Military Policemen. It would be a quick trip for them—less than a mile. As they neared the alley, they dismounted from their vehicles and advanced the rest of the way on foot. Once they reached the entrance to the alley, they deployed on its right side, where they would operate for the duration of the battle, as would Cisneros' forces on the left. The two reaction forces, now two combat elements, were completely unknown to one another. But, they had a common mission, and would work closely and in conjunction with one another. Both sides would endeavor mightily to advance, clear the alley, and reach and evacuate the wounded. Little did they know that it would be a long and very stressful association. They would work together the remainder of the night, all the next day, until the last VC had been eliminated from the alley.

It was astonishing, but most rewarding, for Cisneros and Waltman to have a totally unexpected reaction force and another leader, Captain Drolla, reach the alley and join them. Not too many moments before, Waltman was "sweating out" whether he would have any reinforcements at all join him. Now, unbelievably, there were two reaction forces working side by side.

The enemy must have detected that more troops had arrived, for the moment the first members of QRF #1 were moving forward, they came under withering fire. Their baptism of fire was similar to and as heavy as that received by elements of the MP reaction force just a short time before. The fire that they were receiving seemed to come primarily from a pagoda-type building to the west, and from a couple of buildings to the east. The enemy observation posts were excellent, as were their fields of fire. QRF personnel used rifle fire to try to neutralize the VC, but their efforts were quickly thwarted by heavy grenade and automatic weapons fire. Nevertheless, QRF troops continued with further probes along the alley in an attempt to find possible weak spots in the enemy positions. All their efforts met with discouraging negative results. From the time of their arrival until daylight, QRF elements would be continually subjected to extremely heavy automatic weapons fire, grenades, rockets, and Claymore mines.

Waltman, Cisneros, and Drolla would ride out the remaining hours of the night, hoping and believing that when daylight came, the VC would be gone to continue on their interrupted mission. However, much to their great disappointment, such would not be the case. When dawn came, there was no sign of any withdrawal. The enemy was entrenched as tightly as they had been at the very outset of the action.

For the MPs and HAC personnel, the picture was grim. They would have to continue into the new day the efforts that thus far had been completely and drastically thwarted. Their fundamental mission was not to clear the alley, but to clear enough of the alley so that rescuers could reach the destroyed truck, and evacuate the surviving wounded.

What was so especially exasperating and deeply frustrating—the MPs and HAC's soldiers had already demonstrated the determination, zeal, selflessness, and courage necessary to get the job done. But they were impossibly handicapped. A huge and most formidable obstacle stood squarely in their way.

It was later determined that the obstacle was the VC company that took control of the alley just ahead of the MPs. It was a Reinforced Demolition Company with a hefty arsenal of powerful, deadly weapons—AK-47s, RPGs, Claymores, grenades, and explosives. All of these they had already exhibited and demonstrated so effectively and tellingly in the alley. The company was a major military element that had been organized for a specific purpose, and its members had served together, trained together and they were the first in the alley. They quickly seized the upper floors and roofs of buildings. That would provide them with unlimited observation and excellent fields of fire. At all times they would be looking *down* on the valley.

Facing them and trying to get through them were two reaction forces—together totaling about sixty to seventy men, or about a *quarter of the strength* of the VC company. These were not tactical troops. Half the men in this element had just a few hours before been Military Policemen; the other half until now had been service support type personnel. They had no AK-47s, RPGs, Claymores, explosives. No, what they had were M-14 and M-16 automatic rifles, some hand grenades, some M-79 grenades a very few M-60 machine guns. And in the alley they were at all times looking up.

This is the force that was endeavoring to get through *that* force and on to the truck.

When daylight arrived, two of Lieutenant Cisneros' men who had been wounded during the night by grenades after barely entering the alley, were still pinned down. Cisneros decided that he could not wait any longer to try to extract them. So he sent for the two-and-a-half ton truck that had transported the second reaction force. He informed Captain Drolla of his intentions, and requested that HAC troops cover his movements by pouring fire on the enemy to distract them. Even though they were still under fire, they quickly backed in the truck, placed the wounded on its bed, gunned the engine and flew out to safety. None were hit.

Firing would be continuously exchanged throughout the morning. For reasons just discussed, an impasse had been reached. Our elements just did not have the stuff necessary to blow up and dislodge the enemy. The spirit was willing, but the flesh was weak.

As the action in the alley had unfolded, Lieutenant Colonel George and I had been kept fully abreast of the situation. We agreed that it was now absolutely necessary that we obtain outside help. The best help that we could obtain for this situation would be an armored element with a tank or two. The quickest, most responsive source for what we needed was the ARVN, which had armored elements. It was agreed that George, with his better communications, would contact the CMD (Capital Military District), which controlled the ARVN in Saigon, for immediate help. After some wait, the request was neither acknowledged nor acted upon. No armor from the ARVN.

Near BOQ #3 just inside the JGS Compound, the ARVN had two tanks. Their location placed them only yards away from the action in the alley, where help was urgently needed. They refused to come to our aid, not even with just fire support. No armor from the ARVN.

This was most demoralizing and frustrating for our forces, which were desperately and frantically trying to find a way to reach the voices still crying out with pleas for help. Lieutenant Colonel George and I had great difficulty suppressing our anger. We were fighting what was the ARVN's fight, we were fighting to save their city, and our presence in the alley holding down the VC there was taking some of the heat off their fight in the JGS Compound at Tan Son Nhut. Yet, we were left to our own devices.

Despite the great handicaps they faced, the MPs and HAC troopers refused to hang back. Rather, they still punched along, took great chances, tried to advance, and still drew heavy fire.

* * *

Very early in this text, I mentioned that when HAC was confronted with that formidable, seemingly impossible TET attack challenge, it tapped every possible resource, every asset that it had at its disposal, and threw them into the Battle for Saigon. A prime example of the efforts of a single asset is the story of Sergeant Donald K. Williams. That soldier was a member of Company B, 716th Military Police Battalion. When I assumed command of HAC, Williams, after a screening process, was assigned to me as my driver and bodyguard. He was six-feet, five-inches tall—a highly intelligent, articulate, loyal, selfless soldier, a picture book MP.

As I was sitting at my desk receiving grim reports concerning the tragic situation in the alley, Sergeant Williams, uncharacteristically, burst into my office and stood at attention in front of my desk. Without waiting for me to speak, he informed me that he had been monitoring the MP frequency on the radio, and had learned of the devastating ambush in the alley. He was particularly upset and concerned about the wounded men who were pinned down. Astonishingly, he then asked that I release him so that he could join in the firefight in the alley. My first reaction was to say no, but he was already pleading his case. He stated that the wounded were his fellow MPs, that he just could not sit still in the office while they suffered, and that he wanted desperately to try to do something to help them. With that I gave him my permission to go. He left the office, but almost immediately returned. He said that the fastest way for him to get to the alley was in my car. Could he borrow it? At that point I just could not refuse him, so my own driver and my car would soon be at the scene of the battle. What was quite amazing, Sergeant Williams was not ordered or advised to go; it was not suggested that he go. It was *he* alone who decided to leave the relative safety of the office to engage in a firefight.

I would later learn that at the scene he was like a man possessed, and that for a brief period he engaged in a kind of lone ranger crusade similar to that of Van Wagner, as earlier described. When Williams arrived at the alley, he saw that all the men were pinned down. He watched as several MPs made attempts to move along the alley, saw them forced to retreat under a hail of fire as soon as they showed any part of themselves. He now heard for himself the cries of the wounded, and felt extremely guilty that he could not help them. He was there. He had to do something.

He approached an officer, and was granted permission to try to get on the roof of the building on their side of the alley. The house was across a courtyard from the wall where men were pinned down. A gate was conveniently located in an area that was shielded from the VC line of fire. As Williams was leaving to try to reach the roof, another sergeant asked to accompany him. Now it was a two-man crusade. Two men stood a better chance of getting on the roof, as one could provide cover for the other. The two received small arms fire as they raced across the courtyard, but were not hit. They entered the house through an unlocked door in the rear, and went up to the second floor after checking all the rooms, but encountered no resistance. In an upper room they found a very frightened Vietnamese family huddled together. When asked about VC on the roof, they indicated no VC. When Williams and the sergeant reached the roof, they found a three-foot wall around it. Without the wall to protect them, it would not have been possible for them to remain on the roof, because small arms fire would be popping all around them. The sergeant carried up an M-79 grenade launcher with ammunition that Williams had retrieved at the mouth of the alley. Williams was not familiar with the weapon but the sergeant was. Williams had brought along a M-16 automatic rifle. The sergeant, with his M-79, and Williams, with his M-16, poured fire at the white house across the alley where VC were supposedly located. What they hoped to accomplish was to suppress VC fire across the way, which might make it easier for those on the ground to get closer to the wounded men. After a time, the return fire from across the way had greatly slackened. But now with Williams and the sergeant out of ammunition, they came down off the roof. When Williams returned to the ground, he was told that HAC headquarters had called on his car radio with the information that he was needed at the headquarters and to return at once.

As he departed, Sergeant Williams felt better about himself. He had been tested, and he believed that in the time available he had done all that he could to help his fellow MPs. His only hope was that his efforts, brief as they were, had in some small way helped suppress some enemy fire that would assist the rescue efforts. His experience in the alley, however, left an indelible mark upon him, for from that time on he would always live with the desperate cries that had propelled him into the alley.

★ ★ ★

Now both the MPs and the HAC force decided to go for broke. They began pouring out every bit of fire that they could muster—automatic rifles, the M-79, 40mm grenade launchers, and even some machine guns. They tried to utilize to their best advantage the tree-lined wall that ran on both sides to the top of the alley. This would not be aimed fire. They saw no VC. Rather, it was more like the reconnaissance by fire often used by attacking armor units. They fired at every spot where they believed a VC was hiding—windows, doors, roofs. But the VC were not just hiding—they continued to fire back. For our forces it was pop up, shoot, duck, move, pop up, shoot again.

This must have worked, for it seemed to press back the VC toward a couple of white two story buildings, one on each side of the alley, which together dominated the mouth of the alley.

And then suddenly, out of nowhere, came the big break that they had been hoping and waiting for, perhaps a big turning point in the alley fight. Another dedicated, selfless individual appeared on the scene, and most importantly brought with him two ARVN V-100s, along with a few very reluctant ARVN soldiers. They were low profile, armor-plated, security vehicles. They had two .30 caliber machine guns and a revolving turret, and four doughnut-like tires. This was not exactly the armor that they had earlier requested and hoped for, but this unexpected augmentation gave a real boost to the heavier weapons-starved troops. They had now acquired a new capability at a critical time.

The individual responsible for this significant reinforcement was Major Eugene J. Conner, operations officer of MACV Advisory Team 100. Major Conner, now the senior officer on site, immediately assumed command of the operation. (During the early Battle for Saigon, there would be missing the usual chains of command so familiar within tactical units. Instead, there would be glowing examples of individuals rising to the occasion and displaying dedication, selflessness, initiative, and improvisation. Major Conner was a prime example.)

He, with little delay, developed an attack plan centered around and immediately utilizing his two V-100s. While one of the vehicles would be pouring out suppressive fire from behind the alley wall, the other would move down the alley firing as it went, endeavoring to reach the shattered truck. This vehicle would be followed closely by several troopers, whose job it would be to load the casualties into the V 100 upon reaching the truck. Since the area around the truck had to be secure in order to prepare the wounded for evacuation, virtually the total remaining resources would have to be used in the assault. Major Conner and Lieutenant Waltman would lead the remaining twenty-five MPs in the reaction force along the left side, while Captain Drolla, with about thirty of his HAC personnel, would move his force along the right side. Both elements would attempt to drive out and destroy the enemy from the buildings on their side of the alley.

Both of the attacking forces moved quickly and aggressively

along the tree-lined wall. Then, finally, after hours of desperate, frantic, and frustrating effort, the moment they had been fighting and praying for arrived—they had reached the truck. What confronted them was shocking, stunning, gruesome, and heartrending. Absolutely miraculously, difficult to comprehend, an individual with at least six wounds had somehow been able to roll under parts of the destroyed two-and-a-half ton truck, and had survived twelve hours of great pain and suffering and fire all around him. However, the great joy of participating in this incredible rescue was immediately dampened for all the troops. At once, a pall dropped down over them. It was now perfectly obvious that he was the only survivor. There, stacked on the blown-up truck and scattered randomly around it, were bodies, parts of bodies, steel helmets, fragments of flak jackets. It was a shattering and demoralizing sight for the rescuers. Of the twenty men in the truck—the three in the cab and seventeen in the truck bed—sixteen had been instantly killed or had died from wounds before the rescuers could get to them. As earlier mentioned, three survivors had somehow crawled out of the alley, were taken to BOQ #3, and were later evacuated to a hospital. The individual recovered in the alley was the fourth survivor. He was placed inside the V¬-100, and moved out of the alley for evacuation.

Then, suddenly, pandemonium! Again, seemingly out of nowhere, and as though the VC had gotten their second wind, down poured heavy fire again. There was certainly no "quit" in these tenacious adversaries.

The HAC forces immediately threw it into reverse, and back peddled down the fire swept lane, as did the MP elements across the way. Major Conner, Lieutenant Waltman, and about nine of the MPs who had been nearest the disabled truck rushed for cover. The nearest proved to be a small house that sat next to the two-story building on their side of the alley, which appeared to be jammed with VC. Major Conner stood at the door waiting as members of his force rushed in. With one last look to be sure that they were all in, this great warrior moved to enter the building, and then astonishingly, tragically, he was the victim of a direct hit from one RPG that blew him in two. It was a staggering, stunning blow for this small group to watch as their leader was cut down in such a decisive, horrible manner. Lieutenant Waltman, inside the room, was sent spinning across it by the same blast, with wounds along the left side of his body—left shoulder, arm, and face. Van Wagner, who for several demanding hours had shared so much with Waltman, without hesitation provided first aid to him by wrapping his bloody face with bandages. It was not until he was finished with that task that he realized that he, himself, had been wounded in the left forearm by a fragment from that RPG.

Other casualties included Private First Class Jerome A. Jefferson, who received a fragment that seriously damaged his eye, and an unnamed, unknown senior sergeant who was a member of Major Conner's advisory team. He was standing behind the major, and had his left arm blown off at the shoulder by the RPG round that had killed him.

The confusion lessened and the group settled in a bit, and as Van Wagner gathered himself, he noticed a small hole above him in the roof of the house. He looked up through it, and to his surprise immediately noticed two VC, who were at an open window in the two-story building right next to them. In all the hours in the alley, this was Van Wagner's first clear look at VC. He saw their faces, attire, and then in dismay watched as they fired their AK-47s down the alley. Van Wagner immediately knew that he and the others in the room were in great danger. If he could look up and see the VC, they most certainly could look down and see the little group in the tight confines of the small room. It would be an easy matter for the VC to wipe them out merely with another single rocket propelled grenade. So everyone remained as quiet as they could, even the wounded, and they pressed against the wall of their room, which disconcertingly, to say the least, was the only thing that separated them from the heavily enemy occupied building leaning against them.

The battle in the alley continued. The MP and HAC forces had gotten so very close, but then had been driven back from the destroyed truck; regrettably the bodies on and around it still lay unmoved. It tore the hearts of all the troopers to know that they still were unable to evacuate them.

Because of the serious arms mismatch in the alley, it had earlier been concluded that it was armor that was required to turn the battle around. That was why the pleas to the ARVN had been made; the ARVN were the only ones in town with armor. But, as has already been mentioned, they turned deaf ears to the request, and no armor was forthcoming

But suddenly there was a drastic, totally unexpected development. The very first evidence that tactical troops might soon be arriving to assist in the fight for Saigon revealed itself. An alert MP patrol spotted a column of tactical vehicles moving slowly along the streets of Saigon. The patrol quickly determined that the element was Troop A, 1st Squadron, 4th Cavalry, 1st Infantry Division. Troop A had been given a mission by its squadron that would take it through parts of Saigon. The MP patrol immediately by radio reported this information to Lieutenant Colonel George. In turn George, with great battle sense, directed that the patrol stay along with the unit and keep him informed of that element's progress through the city. He then emphasized that they notify him immediately when elements of "A" Troop reached a point that would put them as close as they were going to get to the fight near BOQ #3. Then they would halt the column, and get the squadron commander on the radio to George.

Very soon, because of his excellent communications capability, George was talking to the Lieutenant Colonel in command, and quickly provided him with a succinct and graphic description of the situation in the alley. He then requested of the commander the "loan," for a very brief period, of a small contingent of armor. Fortunately, there quickly developed a winning combination. Happily, the commander was a can do, will do guy. Lieutenant Colonel George had been an alert opportunist. The commander agreed to provide the armor, and George provided an improvised opportunity to the forces in the alley.

Very soon up rolled two tanks and two APCs (Armored

Personnel Carriers). The armor commander was provided with a quick feel of the situation, and in no time he had a tank and an APC on each side of the alley blasting away. The tanks, firing 90mm, high explosive shells, and the APCs, pouring out a continuous stream of powerful, deadly .50 caliber rounds, together put out an enormous volume of fire. They fired at the tops and sides of the buildings, and just blew the hell out of them. In one fell swoop the worm had made a radical turn. Now at last it was the VC who were outgunned. With walls collapsing around them, they had no place to hide. They could no longer rise up and fire their RPGs and AK-47s. All they could do was run, and all the survivors did just that. It was not long before there was not a VC to be found.

The alley fight was over!

With their job amazingly, quickly, and extremely well done, the small armor detachment withdrew and returned to their unit before darkness settled in.

With the final *boom* of the tank, an eerie silence descended upon the alley.

It was 1700 hours, and the alley was secure at last. That small, tight, unimposing, non-descript piece of inner city terrain had been unspeakably ravished during the last fourteen hours. It was the scene, during that period, of brutal violence and unceasing weapons fire—some very heavy, some lighter, but always fire with no let up. Now suddenly there was none, and a weird feeling came over the no longer embattled troops. They were now free to move around, but their first steps were tentative and hesitant. They seemed to be holding their breaths, waiting for fire to erupt and ready to dive for cover. But there was no more fire. After some minutes had passed and with it a brief period of acclimation, they realized that there was still urgent work to be done and that they had better "get at it."

The first demanding order of business was the extremely difficult, disturbing, sad, grim and gruesome job of recovering the dead and dismembered bodies of their fallen MPs, and evacuating them. For the MPs who undertook this heartrending task, it was profoundly emotional. They were moving mostly unrecognizable individuals with whom they had trained and served, and who had been friends and even buddies. In one fell swoop they were gone—gunned down unmercifully, horribly. The MPs were understandably gravely shaken, and would bear this night's scars for years to come, if not forever.

Fortunately by this time Vo Tanh Street had been cleared and secured between BOQ #3 and the 3rd Field Hospital. For the ambulances and evacuation vehicles, it was a short, straight drive.

The remainder of the troops "policed" the area for scattered weapons and equipment, preparatory to returning to their units and billets. By 1900 hours all MP and HAC elements had been withdrawn, and the alley was completely clear.

After 1900 hours it was just another Saigon alley. Hardly! This one was war torn, demolished. One glance left no doubt but that it was the site of something momentous; a war had been fought there; a tremendous amount of action had taken place within a very small area. No building was unscathed; some had been hit many times in many different ways. Some had hundreds of holes. The floor of the alley was littered with palm fronds. Competing with the fronds were sheets of tin roofing, which also littered the alley. Some palm trees were uprooted; others were left without tops, some mere stumps.

It was a total, complete mess!

Yet, it soon became a mecca for newspaper, magazine, TV writers and cameramen, and the curious. Once the battle for Saigon permitted, visitors to the alley began arriving. They appeared astonished with their first glance at the alley, and awestruck once they were in it. Every visitor would make it a point to stand sadly and soberly at the site of "the truck."

They treated it as hallowed ground, which it was, and will always be.

Observations

1. In addition to the truck casualties, there was one killed and twenty-four reinforcements wounded.

2. Lieutenant Waltman and Specialist Van Wagner were awarded the Silver Star for gallantry in action during the BOQ #3 Battle.

3. The alley battle was a graphic example of the critical importance of tactical weaponry. It emphasized the difficulties and challenges that the MPs and HAC forces faced without them. Those elements endeavored mightily to execute tactical force missions without tactical force weaponry. The tactical weaponry of the VC—AK-47s, RPGs, and Claymores, soundly trumped M-14s and M-16s. Yet it would not be long before the VC were routed, as their tactical weaponry in turn was trumped by heavier tactical weaponry. This came in the form of a tiny armor detachment of two tanks and two armored personnel carriers.

4. The BOQ #3 Battle resulted in many American casualties. Was this a complete setback, or was there something positive that emerged from this fight? If nothing else, the MPs and HAC forces tied down completely a powerful, reinforced company during a very critical period, and inflicted upon them an uncounted number of casualties. Beyond that, there can be only conjecture. The battle for control of the JGS Compound between the VC and ARVN forces lasted all day and was nip and tuck all the way, with the ARVN finally prevailing. If the VC battalion had retained the company that was left behind in the alley and was at full strength, it surely would have had the advantage it needed to win the fight. Since that did not happen, it could be surmised that perhaps by tying up the VC company, the MPs and HAC forces helped save the JGS Compound. Carrying this conjecture a bit further, had the VC captured the JGS Compound, they would have been free to move on to assault other close, important, lucrative targets. MACV Headquarters was not too far away. No, the battle in the alley was a far cry from being a total loss.

Action in the alley.

Concentrated "push" in the alley.

The BOQ #3 alley fight.

Rescue team follows a V-100 security vehicle toward rocket-damaged truck.

"Cleaning up" after the fight.

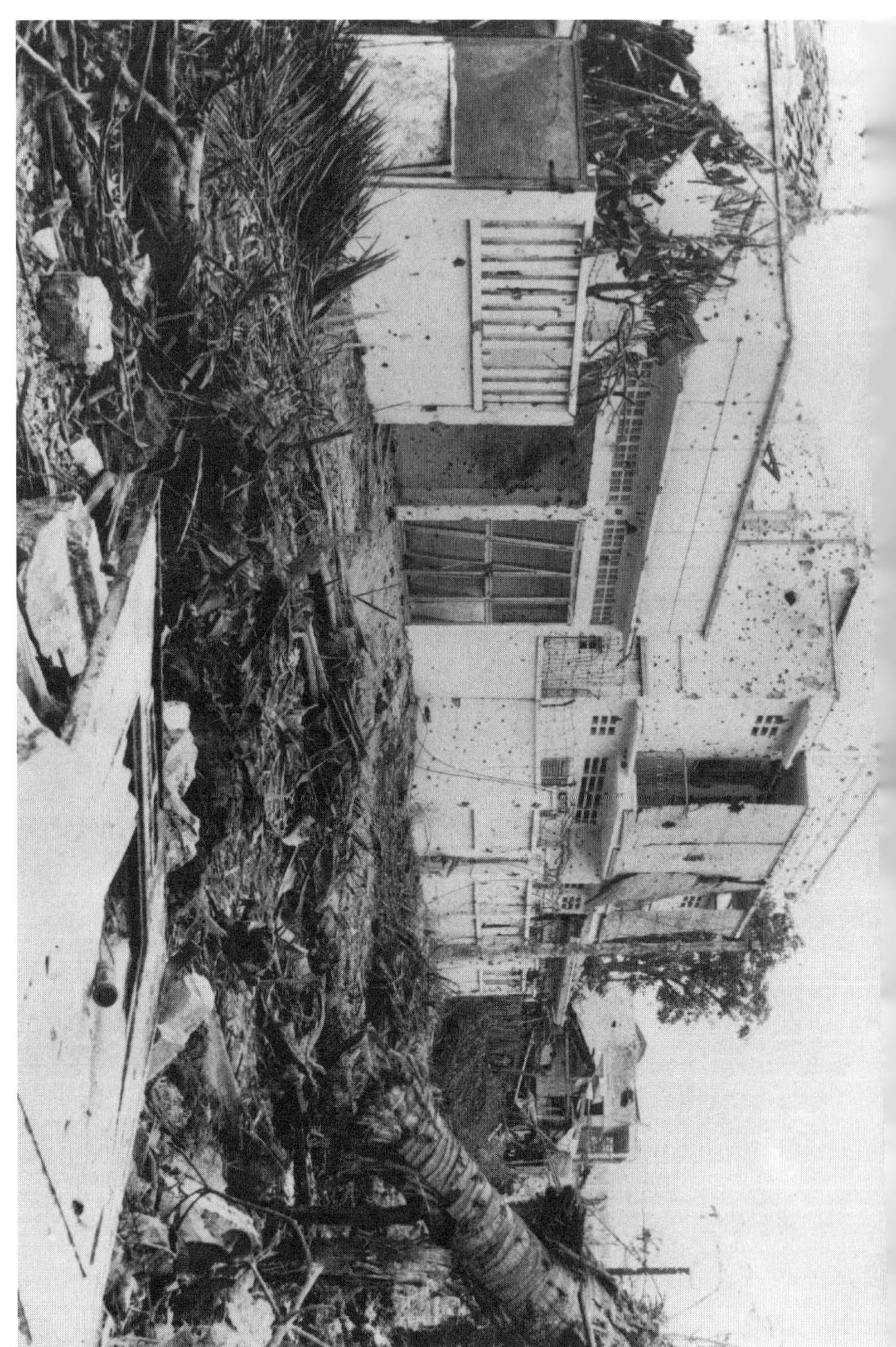

Alley at the end of the fight.

PITCHED BATTLES AND ENGAGEMENTS

CHAPTER 10
THE FIGHT AT THE PHU THO RACETRACK

This is the story of another pitched battle during the early hours of the assault on Saigon. It is the tale of a brief, extremely intense, confusing, inconclusive engagement that mirrored the unpredictable chaos that prevailed among many diversified engagements in many different locations in the city of Saigon. This brief story, like others during the Saigon battle, does not permit a cohesive, flowing account, cannot be told in the descriptive narrative of typical war story. It had unexpected ramifications. Yet, it would turn out to be just a slightly larger blip on the log of citywide Saigon engagements.

The Phu Tho Racetrack, which will be frequently mentioned in this narrative, was a horse racing facility located in the western section of Saigon and was a part of and a kind of gateway to Cholon. Its location placed it at the hub of many streets, at the northwest corner of the north-south Plantation Road. The racetrack was an extremely well known landmark. Every citizen of Saigon knew of it and its whereabouts. This area would be tactically advantageous for the VC. Because it was so well known, it would be a rallying point for the VC from units all over the city. Importantly, if the VC could hold the track complex, they stood a good chance of holding Cholon. Conversely, it would have great strategic and tactical value if U.S. forces controlled it. It was an ideal landing zone for helicopters, and it was an excellent base from which to operate in Cholon.

The fight at Phu Tho began very innocently, a chance encounter. MP Car 95, with a three-man crew, was one of forty-one widespread jeep patrols prowling the many streets in the sprawling city of Saigon. It was way out of the center of the city on Plantation Road near Cholon. Suddenly, at about 0540, the WACO radio net received a terse message reporting that Car 95 had driven into an enemy force. Then there was a hysterical cry, "They got the sergeant in the guts, and the driver is wounded! They're shooting automatic weapons! We are near the racetrack. They're all over the place. The fire is very heavy! We need help now!" After a brief pause, the radio operator reported that they had taken cover behind the wrecked jeep, which had two flat tires, holes in the gas tank, and the windshield was all shot up.

The nearest reaction force to the action was one of HAC's. It was dispatched immediately, and was told to be careful at the first circle, before they reached the racetrack. The MP with the still functioning radio in the demolished jeep reported that RPG fire was now hitting near them.

The HAC reaction force was soon on Plantation Road heading for Car 95. About two and a half blocks before reaching the racetrack, they leapt out of their vehicles and moved forward on foot. The HAC troopers had not gone very far before they were deluged with fire, stopped cold, and unable to reach Car 95. The situation was already beginning to appear desperate. If there was any doubt, that was soon settled. HAC elements, unbelievably, were receiving, of all things, fire from the "friendlies" in the ARVN Compound and from the VC on both sides of the tree-lined road. Up ahead, the jeep that they had set out to rescue now appeared to be a lost cause. It was being consumed by fire. The night was fading, it was just before dawn, but it was still dark. The darkness was a discouraging, dismal, most unsettling backdrop to the jeep, which was burning furiously and brightly. The three-man crew sprawled near the jeep were soon visible. It would later be learned that two of the crew were dead, and the MP who had been on the radio would play dead, and after an excruciatingly long period reminiscent of BOQ #3, would be rescued in good condition.

The HAC force was now caught between fire from grenade launchers and heavy automatic fire from nearby rooftops.

It was perfectly clear that a real emergency situation prevailed near the racetrack, and that reinforcements were required immediately. To meet the escalating confrontations, another reaction force was quickly dispatched to the area. The second reaction force was C52. The personnel were from HAC's Security Guard Company, which had been placed under the operational command of Lieutenant Colonel Rowe, the commander of the 716th MP Battalion. This force had not been sitting at the gate awaiting the starter's gun. It had already been in action. They had been executing their assigned mission of moving around the streets of Saigon suppressing firefights at various installations like BOQs and BEQs. This force had already been pinned down briefly by the VC during a firefight at the Butte BOQ. They had routed the enemy force and were about to continue on their mission when they received the call to move to the racetrack to render assistance to the HAC reaction force and Car 95, and it soon sped off to try to do just that.

This second reaction force was led by First Lieutenant Stephen L. Braddock. Braddock wanted to be sure that he was heading in the proper direction, to the proper place, so he asked the HAC commander for directions. He was told to turn right at the ARVN compound, that the HAC force was about two blocks beyond, that because of grenade launchers most of his force was spread out behind white water barrels, and that his two-and-a-half ton truck was in the road. Braddock was warned that as he neared his destination his troops should dismount and continue their advance on foot. As he was finishing his report, the HAC commander tersely stated that the enemy was now trying to zero in on them with grenade launchers, and that the situation was becoming even hotter. Braddock assured the HAC commander that C52 was well on the way, bringing him needed help.

It was frustrating and most unfortunate, but C52 never made it.

As it was moving to assist the HAC forces, the VC had slipped in behind the pinned down HAC troops, and now presented a formidable barrier. Braddock, of course, was unaware of this most recent development, had no opportunity to size up the situation, so continued to march.

As recommended by the HAC commander, he had members of C52 dismount and move in a line of skirmishers up the street in the direction of Car 95. The group reached a point about half a block from the corner, and immediately noted two MP bodies lying beside their jeep. Apparently the two individuals were members of an MP jeep patrol, had heard 95's distress call, and had rushed to the scene. They arrived just before the reaction force, and had run into the same ambush that the reaction force had just now hit. All at once heavy fire came from several directions. The fire was so hot that it immediately pinned down the elements of the reaction force. After a time, and still under fire, they were somehow able to extricate themselves, and before becoming serious casualties moved into the safety of a small, handy hotel, where they would stay briefly while planning their next move.

Specialist Max Whitmeyer, one of the leaders of the group, as he was ducking inside the building, gave the outside a final look, and watched in horror and dismay as a two-and-a-half ton truck was hit by rockets, and instantly became a flaming torch, after an explosion.

That truck was the one that had transported C52 to the racetrack area. Lieutenant Braddock had pushed it as far forward as he believed safety would permit, and he hovered near the truck, as it gave him his communications capability. Tragically, when the truck was hit, so was he, and he died instantly. Frustratingly, despite his great effort, the best he could do was to get within two blocks of the firefight that he had rushed to assist. Unaware that Braddock was already dead, an officer and two non-commissioned officers were wounded in a valiant and courageous effort to reach Braddock.

The fight for Saigon was replete with tales of individual heroism, courage, and initiative. Private First Class Dennis Darling and a companion who were members of the C52 Reaction Force were prime examples. They had been on the truck moving from place to place with their unit. As previously mentioned, C52 had a firefight and were pinned down briefly at the Butte BOQ. When they were ordered to move to the racetrack without delay, the troops mounted up hurriedly, and the truck took off abruptly and swiftly. In the confusion Darling and his companion were somehow left behind when the truck pulled out. Undaunted, they did not hesitate a second before moving out on foot to try to catch up with the rest of C52.

Most fortunately, some time after they began their long trek, a speeding MP jeep heading for Car 95 stopped and picked them up. They soon reached the area of conflict, and noted up ahead what appeared to be a truck ablaze. The two left the jeep and began to move forward on foot. As with all others before them, they began receiving enemy fire. In order to close up to where they believed the rest of their team was located, they moved along the street from tree to tree. At the intersection they ran out of trees. As they started to cross the street, they spotted five or six individuals moving up the side street. Darling thought that they were ARVN soldiers, because they had an American M-60 machine gun. But as they got closer, it was obvious that they were VC, for they were also carrying AK-47s and rockets. Darling and his companion opened up very effective fire, and the enemy group immediately broke up and scattered. By this action Darling and his companion were later credited with blocking an enemy encirclement of a pinned down group of members of their C52 unit.

Like all before them, although willing, it was not possible to advance any further. They began looking for a place that would provide them with a good defensive position. Hunkered down, they turned into the next side street, and immediately recoiled in horror. Facing them was what appeared a mass of bodies. There were three dead VC surrounded by puddles of blood, a dead American who had been shot in the face, and a dead ARVN sitting in a jeep. Amazingly and incongruously, among the pile of bodies were two *mamasans* (mothers), their children and a pile of belongings. It appeared that they had been trying to flee and were caught in the middle of heavy crossfire.

The situation had become so desperate that a third reaction force was dispatched and reached the embattled area. Like all the other elements that had been committed to that location, it too was stopped cold, could not move forward. The main reason soon became clear when the HAC commander reported via his radio that, "The VC have about a block section of this street sealed off. We can't move in any direction. They're at both ends, and it's pretty much a stalemate." They were totally and completely boxed in, could not advance nor extricate themselves. What made matters even worse, mortar rounds began dropping in.

It was now perfectly evident that the "innocent, chance encounter" of Car 95 was anything but! It was more like hitting a combination buzz saw and hornet's nest, and then some. Car 95's great crime was getting too close to the Phu Tho Racetrack and posing a perceived threat to it.

There was no question that the VC desperately required the Phu Tho complex. As has been pointed out, the racetrack, for many reasons, was tactically and strategically of vital importance to them. It would be the rallying point for VC units. But the great and overriding reason would not be known until after TET. Here's the big one: Major General Tran Do's command post, from which he controlled the entire Saigon operation, was entrenched in tunnels and bunkers in a cemetery adjacent to the Phu Lam pagoda, only three kilometers west of the racetrack in a rice paddy fringe of Saigon.

No wonder the VC had erupted so fiercely when Car 95 appeared on the scene. Car 95 and the reaction forces that closely followed it had amazingly stumbled onto an area occupied by a regimental command post and two VC battalions, which among other missions undoubtedly had the responsibility of protecting General Do, his staff, and command post.

What was truly impressive was that the tiny, non tactical MP and HAC reaction force, against that powerful element, were able to hang in there. The "chance encounter" at the very least bogged down the enemy, upset their plans, and provided them with a new and unexpected mission.

When the VC assaulted Saigon without tactical troops in town, HAC, by using every resource available, hoped to hang in there, hold onto and save Saigon until the tactical troops could arrive to take over. The fight at Phu Tho was a classic example of that occurring.

The 3rd Battalion, 7th Infantry Regiment, 199th Light Infantry Brigade was commanded by Lieutenant Colonel John Gibler. It was one of the closest battalions ringing Saigon. That battalion was based at Binh Chanh, a small village about thirty miles southwest of the heart of Saigon. Lieutenant Colonel Gibler had carefully watched intelligence reports, and on the eve of TET had an uneasy feeling that something might soon happen. He told his operations officer, Major James Mac Gill, to issue orders to every company to return to the firebase. Thus, they were soon in an excellent state of readiness in the event a call would come. That call did come, and even much earlier than they had expected. Because of their state of readiness and relatively close proximity to Saigon, they were probably the first tactical unit to enter Saigon. When they reached the city the next afternoon, they had already zeroed in on Cholon and Phu Tho.

After pushing through parts of Cholon, they reached a point about six blocks from the racetrack. The VC were ready for them. An enemy soldier fired a rocket-propelled grenade at the incoming convoy. It streaked ominously through the air, and made a direct hit at the lead armored personnel carrier. The front of the APC exploded and sent dust and debris in all directions. Instantly killed were the cavalry platoon leader and two of his men. Only a second later the force was showered with small arms fire. The enemy seemed to be everywhere, and the fire was coming from both sides of the street. Welcome to Pho Tho! The cavalry/infantry force had barely shown itself when its nose was badly blunted, and the lead element already counted three dead. The 3rd of the 7th now knew without any doubt that it was facing anything but a token force, and that it would have a real battle on its hands.

For more than two hours the 3rd of the 7th, a most potent force, hauled up and threw out everything it had at the VC. It went through ammunition magazines in a flash as it fired its machine guns at full automatic. It repeatedly called upon its powerful 106-mms. All this firepower enabled them to slowly advance for about five blocks. Now only a little more than a block away, the VC resistance stiffened even more. The VC were well entrenched in defensive positions. They sprayed the area with more and heavier machine guns. VC machine gunners added more firepower from a building that covered every approach to the racetrack. Frustrated and exhausted, Americans withdrew for a temporary break into buildings near the track.

As a bit of a lull seemed to have descended upon the warring troops, Major Mac Gill, the operations officer, who had been airborne in his command helicopter, landed on a nearby rooftop, which put him just behind some positions held by MPs. He spotted two MPs firing at VC across the street. Mac Gill quickly jumped out of his helicopter and moved down along the street to join them, carrying ammunition for their M-60 machine gun, and watched as they shot at and occasionally hit VC running among the buildings across the way. Major Mac Gill saw a VC come out of a building, hide his rifle, remove a red arm band that identified him, and raise his arms, so as to pass for a civilian about to surrender. Without hesitation, the major aimed his rifle and squeezed the trigger—one less VC to be concerned about.

When Major Mac Gill fired that shot, it was a most significant, symbolic moment. That one shot from an MP position signified that the tactical reinforcements had arrived to take over the battle, and that for HAC's MPs and reaction forces the fight for Phu Tho was over. Most significantly, it was a clear indication that those troops had done their job, and they could proudly say that they had accomplished their mission.

Now, again, symbolically, the time had come for the passing of the baton, the changing of the guard. The 3rd Battalion, 7th Infantry was taking over the fight; it was now theirs.

With some difficulty the HAC forces, almost individually, were able to disengage and withdraw. Once mounted in their vehicles, they reported their availability, and very soon resumed their mission of helping protect and secure the many installations for which HAC was responsible, and protecting, and securing, the very many individuals for whom HAC was also responsible.

For the 3rd of the 7th, the task confronting them proved to be most difficult. For five dirty, exhausting days, from the third to the seventh of February, they slowly but persistently cleaned the VC out of Cholon. The fight for total control of the racetrack complex ebbed and flowed during those days. It was not until February 11, that the final attack at Phu Tho was launched by the American forces. It remained a bloody, dirty, difficult proposition. The VC were still stubborn, would not quit. While surrounding the enemy headquarters, the fighting proved particularly vicious. Finally, with the VC boxed in, gun ships chewed up their bunkers, and their resistance ended. This final battle came at a great cost to the 3rd of the 7th. Six cavalry/infantry troopers were killed and fourteen wounded.

Radios, documents and much miscellany were captured along with four VC. Strewn around the battle area were forty-nine dead enemy fighters. There was no sign of General Do.

The fight for the Phu Tho Racetrack, which began during the early hours of January 31, was finally over.

During those early hours, in addition to HAC casualties, five MPs were killed and twelve wounded.

PITCHED BATTLES AND ENGAGEMENTS

CHAPTER 11
HAC REACTION FORCE ENGAGEMENTS

Quick Reaction Force #1

This platoon-sized reaction force was heavily involved and totally committed at the BOQ #3 fight along with the MPs.

Quick Reaction Force #2

The main transportation motor pool of HAC, the largest non tactical, administrative motor pool in the U.S. Army worldwide, was located near the Phu Tho area close to Cholon. During the early hours of January 31, it had its usual, small nighttime security force on duty consisting of two U.S. soldiers, four ARVN soldiers, and five Vietnamese security guards. However, because of its extensiveness, locality, and vital importance, QRF #2 was dispatched to it as soon as the magnitude of the attack was recognized. The reaction force immediately established a formidable defensive perimeter.

Not long in coming was heavy enemy automatic weapons fire, which would continue. Soon after, the motor pool received a small two-pronged attack, which was successfully repelled, and the enemy scattered. One VC was killed, one wounded, and three abandoned their weapons and satchel charges. For four days the troops inside the motor pool would periodically receive small arms and heavy automatic weapons fire. At 1630 on February 1, mortar and rocket fire suddenly hit close in. An ARVN sergeant at the main gate was hit above the right eye, and died shortly after he was evacuated. HAC forces successfully defended that important installation, and suffered no casualties.

Quick Reaction Force #3

Located near downtown Saigon on Hieu Vuong Street was a sub-motor pool. Because ARVN and Vietnamese security guards were not available early on January 31, ten enlisted U.S. personnel, mostly drivers and mechanics, and one sergeant were on duty. Shortly after the assault on Saigon began, sporadic rifle fire was received in the motor pool. More accurate and more deadly sniper fire began to be received from at least three locations. One VC was killed while attempting to force his way into the motor pool, and one was wounded and captured. Three more were soon captured near the main gate.

Then, suddenly, the enemy began heavily mortaring the motor pool. Their positions were directly across the street. Since the situation was now becoming tense, QRF #3, a smaller reaction force, was dispatched. It arrived quickly, and once inside the motor pool, more than doubled the force, and brought a substantial increase in firepower. This was immediately concentrated on the mortar locations, which were subsequently eliminated.

The successful and stalwart defense of the HAC transportation motor pools preserved more than fifty million dollars worth of valuable property, which included many hundreds of vehicles that would soon be called upon to resume the tremendous logistical support for beleaguered Saigon.

Quick Reaction Force #4

It was personnel of the U.S. commissary and the U.S. army clothing sales store, together numbering about thirty individuals, who made up this reaction force. It was commanded by the clothing sales officer, who was a member of HAC's staff. Their prime mission was to defend a compound known as COFAT. To ensure security they established a perimeter defense with some guard posts. COFAT was the location of a number of key installations, among them the commissary, the clothing sales store, and the U.S. Post Office, which was operated by the Air Force. All of these facilities contributed greatly to the day-to-day existence and well being in Saigon of very many Americans and allied individuals.

The VC made no attempt to assault the compound, and it was never penetrated. From the outset, however, small arms and automatic weapons fire was received. This would continue sporadically during January 31 and February 1. Additionally, there were instances when more accurate, troubling sniper fire came inside the compound, which caused personnel who were moving around to scurry to a safe place. The defenders were able to find and kill one sniper. That was the only casualty at COFAT.

QRF #4's contribution to the events in Saigon was twofold. First, it protected and secured a tremendously important and valuable installation. Second, it provided a safe haven for a large number of people in trouble. Individuals who were endangered and sought refuge in a safe place, like individuals from the American Medical Association, were directed by the Provost Marshal to try to reach COFAT for protection. Many followed his instructions. The number who responded would reach 275 by the second day. Fortunately, because the commissary was within the compound, all those individuals were provided subsistence during the time that they remained at that location.

Task Force Charlie

While the fighting was heavy at BOQ #3, an area known as the MACV Annex, just north of the JGS Compound, came under attack from a sizeable element spilling over from the very large, heavy force that was moving against the Tan Son Nhut Air Base from the north. To meet the smaller force, Task Force Charlie, made up of HAC personnel like finance clerks (34th and 10th Finance Sections) and drivers, deployed to defensive positions on the civilian golf course adjacent to the air base. Tan Son Nhut soon came under heavy ground attack. Simultaneously, enemy automatic weapons and mortar fire was brought to bear against Gate 10 to the north of the air base, and near where Task Force Charlie had deployed. This was a critical location. The fire from the attacking enemy, including AK-47s and RPGs, intensified. The HAC forces fought valiantly and tenaciously to hold their positions and prevent an enemy penetration. By now every clerk, mechanic, driver, and postal clerk available to the HAC task force commander had been committed to the defense of Gate 10. As time passed, the fire became even heavier, and it appeared that the HAC positions were about to be overrun. To stabilize the situation, reinforcements from somewhere were desperately needed. Then, once again in the very nick of time, after HAC had once again been able to hang in there, some troops were diverted from a column of the 25th Division passing through, and helped immensely to turn the tide.

By its actions Task Force Charlie played a significant role in helping keep secure, not only the MACV Annex and Gate 10, but the nearby and huge MACV compound, as well.

Additionally

In addition to HAC's named and numbered reaction forces, which had been constituted from HAC's personnel resources, there were smaller quick reaction forces that secured, and when necessary, defended HAC's installations, which were scattered around the city.

THE PLAYERS

CHAPTER 12
CONDUCT OF THE BATTLE FOR SAIGON
DIMINUTIVE BUT TREMENDOUS

A century after the American Revolution, Sir George Otto Trevelyan would write in a classic study of our early history about the battle at Trenton: "It may be doubted whether so small a number of men ever employed so short a space of time with greater and more lasting effects upon the History of the World."

It had happened before in military history. A relatively unnoticed, unheralded element, just minding its own business, is suddenly confronted with an extremely grave and totally unexpected emergency. A catastrophe apparently far beyond its capability to avert is unfolding. Something must instantly be done to avoid disaster. And it is the only element available to do any "doing."

Out of nowhere and without hesitation, a group or individual leaps headlong at the challenge. It is much like the guy who with a superhuman, Herculean effort lifts the car long enough so that the body pinned underneath can be dragged to safety. A very small element scores a tremendous victory. Its totally unexpected and effective actions, greatly out of proportion with its size and capabilities, turns the tide, averts the catastrophe, and "saves the day."

Such is the story of HAC during the battle for Saigon during TET of 1968 when the Communists attacked that capital city.

HAC was the only U.S. Army headquarters in town. It was there only to provide support and protection on a daily basis to the thousands of Americans and allies who worked and lived in the city. It had not been organized, established, or placed in the city with a *com-*

bat mission included among its many assigned tasks. Such a mission for it had been far beyond consideration.

Yet, on the morning of January 30, 1968, when General Westmoreland perceived a genuine threat to Saigon and in the total absence of U.S. Army tactical troops and tactical headquarters, and certainly with a degree of desperation, it was the HAC command and I that he called upon for help. At that point, with no one else to turn to, he, in essence, placed the responsibility for the defense of Saigon squarely upon my shoulders. Realizing that, it was for me a most sobering moment.

From the time of the Westmoreland telephone call until the waning afternoon hours, every preparatory resource, every possible individual had been put in place. At that point the total available *combat* assets of HAC had locked arms, and that organization was as prepared as it could possibly be for whatever adversity it might be called upon to face the next day. The command was "at the ready."

The threat turned out to be far more massive than anyone could possibly have imagined or foreseen. The performance of HAC, likewise, was far beyond anything that could have been expected of it.

For the next many hours, the members of the HAC command engaged in and carried out a myriad of missions that they had never expected, encountered, experienced, and for which they had never been trained, equipped, or mentally or psychologically prepared.

The battle for Saigon was anything but a conventional city battle, such as have been recounted in many history books. In a war, advancing forces that find a city in their way will exert every possible effort to bypass the city. The last thing any offensive army wants is the requirement to fight its way through a large city. When such a battle for a city does occur, history records face offs between two uniformed adversaries. Here the battlefield is relatively small, tight, and very restricted. The advantage is to the defender who knows the city, and is able to pick the best spots from which to fight. The attackers, with pistols, rifles, grenades, are forced to fight from house to house, street to street, block by block. The defender, with pistols, rifles, grenades, and booby traps, tries desperately to hold on to every house, street, block. Such battles are slow, painstaking, methodical, dangerous, and deadly.

The battle for Saigon did not in any way, not even remotely, resemble that conventional scenario for a battle for a city. The battle for Saigon was absolutely unique. Because of a strange, unrelated collection of factors, it could never again be repeated, and would always remain one of a kind.

That battle did not have two opposing forces in combat military attire. One force had military uniforms, but only partially combat uniforms. The other was mostly attired in ordinary, everyday Vietnamese street or working clothes. For them there was not a steel helmet or flak jacket to be seen. However, they had the latest military weapons—rifles, pistols, hand grenades, rocket propelled grenades, explosives, and more. The attackers were composed of little people who were quick, sneaky, devious, elusive. They were anything but a tightly organized, concentrated military force. They were not attacking the city in a methodical manner. There was no house-to-house fighting. They attacked many buildings, but did so randomly without coordination. There were many simultaneous skirmishes, many hit, run, hide, pop up, hit again attacks. If they found a vulnerable target, they would attack it and hang in there until flushed out. If they approached a target and found it to be held, they would quickly move on to find something more vulnerable. There was no discernable pattern to their movements. All in all, the battle for Saigon will always remain a classic.

How did HAC fight this totally unexpected, unconventional battle? How did we at HAC "save the day?"

Being very familiar with an army division, I quickly decided, during our planning, that I would pattern our organization after a division. So we fought, in a sense, as a combat division. Of course, our division would, because of its extremely limited size and capabilities, be a miniaturized version of a full division. I would be the commanding general, the overall commander. Every division has elements under its direct control. My headquarters would have elements under its direct control. These were the HAC personnel who would be members of the reaction forces and quick reaction forces. They would be considered my division special troops.

I had but one major tactical commander. He was my Provost Marshal, Lieutenant Colonel George. The Provost Marshal Compound would be my tactical headquarters. Colonel George's desk in the huge, complex city of Saigon had always been a hot spot. It was he who normally was the first to receive word of a serious incident or emergency, and would instantly do something about it. During his time behind that desk, he had already experienced a broad, varied gamut of incidents and emergencies, including terrorist attacks. Saigon was anything but a quiet city. Thus, he had long since received and weathered his baptism of fire. He was solid, steady, unflappable. He coolly handled hot problems. He made quick decisions, and the actions he took were invariably appropriate, pertinent, and effective. There is no question that he was a vitally important member of our organization. In this situation he was well nigh indispensable. He was as well prepared as any individual could have been to meet the TET challenge.

Making him an even more potent force was his great communications capability. He, like we at HAC headquarters, had an extensive telephone network that reached out to every element and location of significance in Saigon and its environs. Additionally, his office was WACO net control. That was the military police radio network. It provided him with the capability of reaching any and all military police elements as required, and all MP elements could reach him, as well. Also included among his communications assets was the ability to reach certain tactical army elements outside of Saigon.

I also had but one combat troop commander. He was Lieutenant Colonel Rowe. He commanded the 716th MP Battalion, had attached to him the 527th MP Company, and had operational command of the HAC Security Guard Company.

Like Lieutenant Colonel George, Lieutenant Colonel Rowe had already experienced and been exposed to every bad and dangerous thing that Saigon had to offer. He was much closer to the actual action than Lieutenant Colonel George, and to the individuals involved in the action. It was the MPs and security forces that he commanded who were spread out all over Saigon and Cholon. It was these young soldiers who were on the front lines that were in constant close contact with the populace of Saigon on a day-to-day basis. They were the first to confront an incident, an emergency, a terrorist attack. They took immediate action. If the situation was too big for them to handle, they would radio for reinforcements, which would almost immediately be on the way.

So he and his forces, like Lieutenant Colonel George, had experienced it all, and had long since had their baptism of fire. He operated under constant, never-ending pressure. Something could pop up at any moment, and invariably did. He and his MPs had always been under constant close scrutiny, as well. The MP uniform was the best-known, most visible item in all of Saigon. His MPs had a tough job to do, and they had performed admirably. They were well trained, disciplined, confident of their abilities, and had high morale.

Because they had been placed on high alert, the MPs, during the last hours of January 30 and the first couple of hours of January 31, were operating on the streets of Saigon in greater strength and a more heightened wariness than was normal. Thus, when the VC came flooding into the city, the MPs were not completely surprised, but they were stunned and astonished by the totally unexpected magnitude of what was unfolding before them. Importantly, they were not entirely "caught short." Instead, they immediately began performing in the usual dedicated, professional, courageous manner, but on a scale never before imagined. They were now aware that they had been engulfed by VC. It would not be an incident here or one there. Almost instantaneously, the MPs and all elements of HAC would be endeavoring to juggle six balls with one hand.

The forty-one widely spread MP jeep patrols had been prowling the streets of Saigon during the midnight hours. During the darkness of those hours, a slippery, slithering adversary in civilian attire had sneaked into the city. Soon a multitude of buildings were being fired upon. In no time many of the jeep patrols became fully engaged with the totally unexpected enemy. The moment an MP element was in enemy contact, it reported as soon as it could the situation by radio to its battalion headquarters. Some of these small patrols quickly met situations that were too hot to handle, and requested immediate assistance. In no time appropriate reaction forces would be dispatched by battalion from the MPs International Hotel to add muscle to the engaged jeep patrols, and to meet the increasing threats that were popping up all over the city. Because the Vietnam citizenry were tightly closed up in their homes, anything moving on the streets not in uniform now became fair game and would instantly be fired upon.

Information of such enemy contact would be sent by the 716th at once to the Provost Marshal, Lieutenant Colonel George, who may already have heard it on his radio. He in turn would immediately pass the information on by telephone to HAC headquarters. Thus, the decision makers were coordinated, unified and on top of the situation. Importantly, we were all "singing from the same sheet of music."

For the attackers there were targets aplenty. HAC alone operated seventy-eight hotels. There was a great miscellany of other HAC targets: motor pools, post engineer facilities, utility installations, warehouses, dining locations, civilian personnel office, a post office and more.

Additionally, there was a whole host of other lucrative targets all over the city for which HAC did not have on a day-to-day basis any direct responsibility. Ambassador Bunker and other senior governmental officials, for example, occupied villas within the city. There was, as well, a broad galaxy of U.S. agencies that occupied a variety of installations. Thus, the enemy had a whole basketful of lucrative targets. All of these were vulnerable, and many would be threatened.

It would soon be obvious that the attackers had no firm plan, little coordination, and only a few pre planned, specific installations to seize. Their overall mission, it seemed, was to reach out and grab quickly as much as they could throughout the night, and to hang on to it until daybreak. As has been mentioned, they, of course, had expected to do this with little ARVN opposition. To their great surprise, shock, and dismay they would have a fight on their hands everywhere they went, and from a totally unexpected source.

So there was bound to have been great confusion in the ranks of the VC. Theirs was a daunting task. It had been mentioned that some of the VC had lived and worked in the city, but the majority came into the huge, complex city as complete strangers in the dark of night. As has also been mentioned, in city fighting, the advantage goes to the defender. In this situation the defenders were the MPs and the HAC reaction forces; they had the advantage. The MPs had crossed and crisscrossed the city over and over, and were most familiar with it. When forces would be dispatched, there was no delay. They could head immediately to the street, intersection, or square where their commitment was required. They would approach an area under fire with caution, and would use to their advantage side streets, alleys and backyards. This would enable them in many instances to corner and surround an enemy element.

Individuals all over town were in a situations that they had not only never experienced, but which they could not even in their wildest dreams ever imagine or expect would happen to them.

The entire gamut of human emotions was instantly on display. There was fright, fear, anger, frustration, desperation, panic, unreasonableness, and recklessness. And, yes, there was, as well, calmness, coolness, selflessness, leadership, self sacrifice, and much courage.

It did not take long after the enemy had made his presence felt that the Provost Marshal and HAC headquarters were inundated with telephone calls. Initially, the calls were all pleas for help. Soon calls would come in with requests and demands for information. The callers for help pleaded for instant assistance. The help they needed invariable required MPs. The calls for MPs would be never ending. As they came in, Lieutenant Colonel George had to weigh each call, make an instantaneous assessment of the request and determine its validity, seriousness, and urgency. He would make a quick decision about the kind and extent of the assistance required.

He would then contact Lieutenant Colonel Rowe and describe

the critical situations. Together they would discuss and agree upon the action to take and what forces to employ. Once the decision was made the reaction forces would soon be on their way. This procedure of thinking, discussing, deciding, was rapid, without delay. Colonels George and Rowe had done such before.

Desperate callers finding the PM lines all tied up would immediately call HAC. The calls to HAC headquarters however were not only those that had initially gone to the Provost Marshal. No! In addition, HAC was beset with calls directed to me. Those were from individuals who chose not to go to the Provost Marshal but to bypass him. Those were calls from self styled movers and shakers who were accustomed to going to the top and becoming a priority. In this situation, I was the "top." I was their last chance.

There was nowhere to go beyond me. As the calls came in, my operations staff screened them. The necessary, urgent ones were immediately passed on for action to the Provost Marshal. Regardless of how dire the need or how critical the emergency, the HAC staff never bypassed Lieutenant Colonel George to go directly to Lieutenant Colonel Rowe for a troop commitment. We were organized, had a chain of command, and we adhered strictly to it.

There were calls and requests that the HAC staff deemed "too hot to handle," and turned them directly over to me. Those came from ranking diplomatic and other senior U.S. officials, generals, senior allied individuals, established newspaper and TV personalities. Each one had a special need and request, which he determined demanded my personal attention and action for him. Meeting these requests under the circumstances then prevailing was way beyond impossible. The worthy, urgent ones I passed on to Lieutenant Colonel George with my recommendations. There were many calls that were inappropriate, unreasonable, did not approach an emergency, or were beyond our capabilities. Consequently, those had to be turned down. Unfortunately, certain of those turn downs were accepted anything but gracefully. Protocol, manners, acceptance of the situation, explanations went out the window. I was amazed and surprised at how the colors changed on certain individuals when they became desperate. When informed that Lieutenant Colonel George and I were not able to meet their requests, they challenged our decisions and remained insistent and demanding. Some were so exasperated that we were even bullied and threatened. Lieutenant Colonels George, Rowe and I had a war to fight. It was certainly not helpful to have such unpleasant diversions.

The calls to the Provost Marshal and to HAC headquarters were unrelenting, and there was never a pause in the requests and demands for Rowe's MPs.

And so it would go for many hours.

In this war there were no measurable miles gained, no towns seized, no high ground successfully assaulted, no bridges overrun. But in this war many buildings, installations, and, much more importantly, many lives would be saved, and so would Saigon.

HAC had hung in there.

★ ★ ★

Excerpt of comments made by Brigadier General Albin F. Irzyk, Commanding General, United States Army Headquarters Area Command during a staff conference on February 8, 1968:

> *. . . Our front line troops were the MPs. They were magnificent, superb. Any superlative one can think of could be applied to the MPs. They were simply magnificent. You cannot realize how many requests came in for their services. Everyone, it seemed, was under fire; everyone was under attack. The MPs were going in dozens of directions at the same time. That battalion was like a rubber band that was stretched to the limit. Not only were they a truly outstanding MP battalion, but they were an outstanding tactical battalion as well.*
>
> *. . . So we defended Saigon; the MPs backed up by the HAC reserves. But we did more. The MPs were engaged in tactical skirmishes doing tactical jobs that were far beyond their mission, simply because there wasn't anyone else to do them. The result: we had no installations lost or damaged, no key individuals lost. As far as Saigon is concerned, we accomplished our mission. We had always been prepared for reaction to terrorist attacks; maybe a bomb at a hotel or two*

bombs at two hotels, a few people throwing hand grenades, or a group of people shooting small arms, hit and run attacks, but never in our wildest imagination did we expect such a widespread attack of such magnitude, of such strength.

This command is a support type command, but for many hours it was the only tactical command in town. It accomplished its tactical mission, which it inherited, because there was no one else to do the job. That is the combat side of HAC . . .

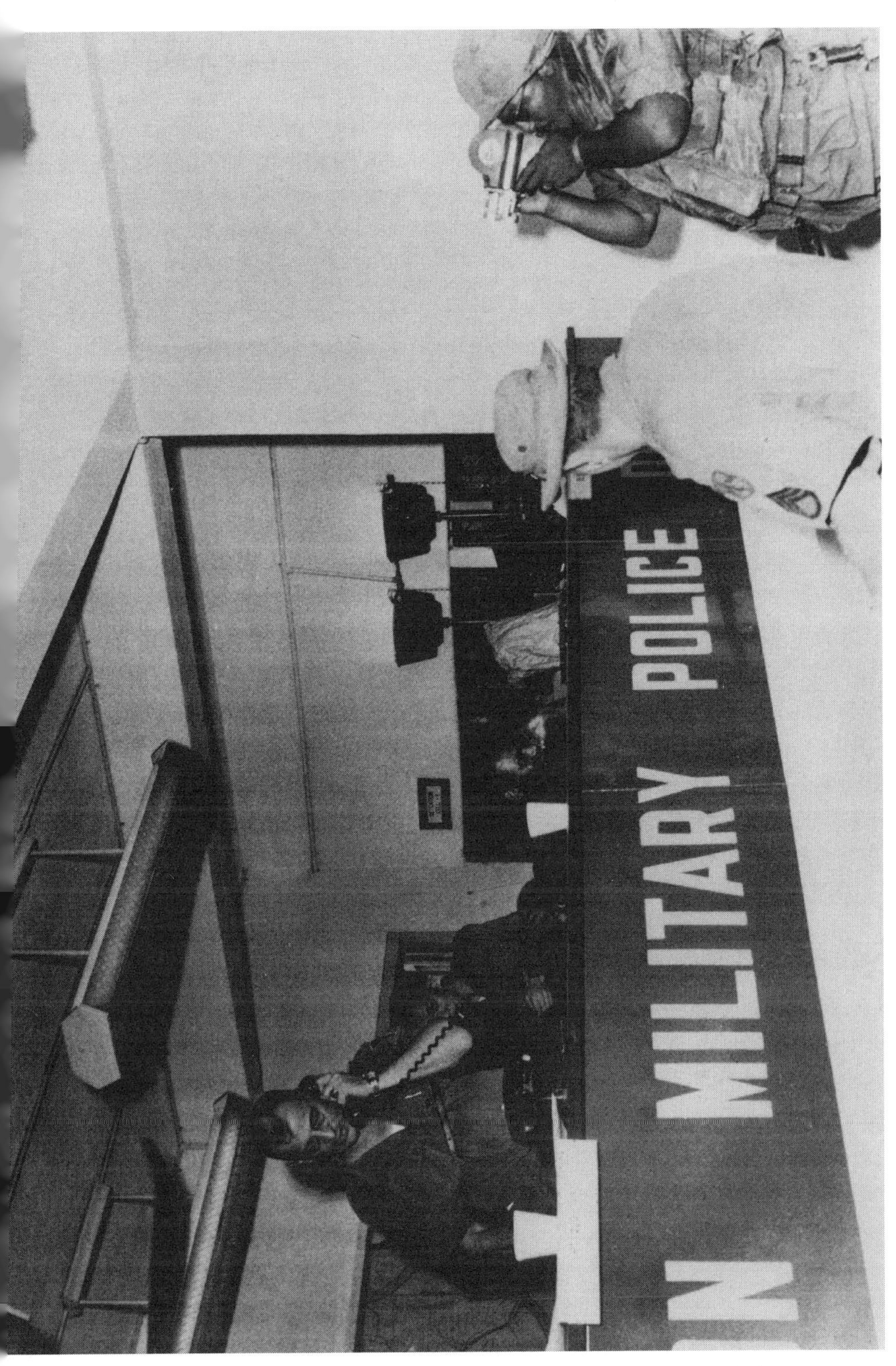

Provost Marshal, Lt. Col. Richard E. George mans the critical desk.

The author and members of his indispensable "right arm."

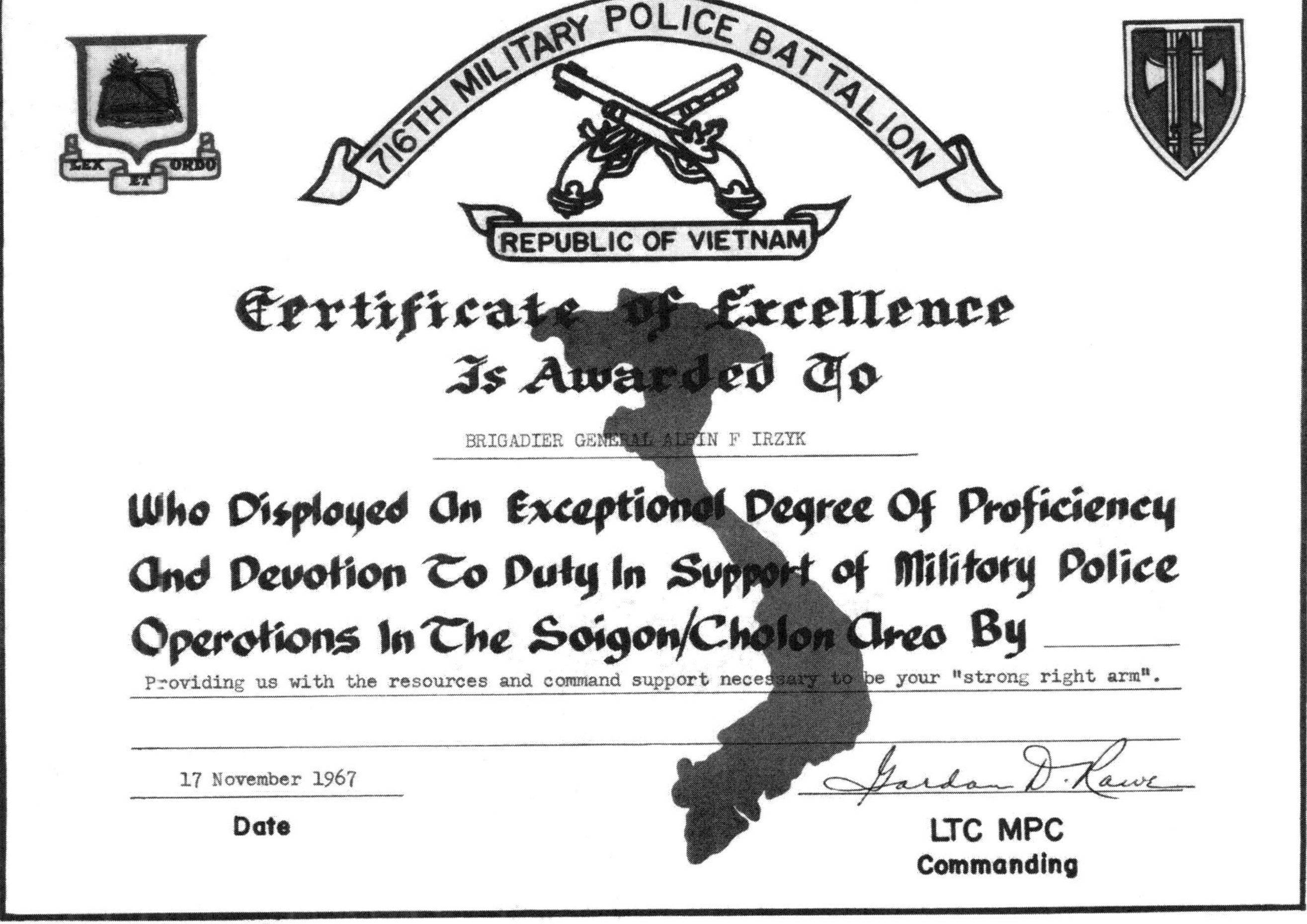

LEX ET ORDO

716TH MILITARY POLICE BATTALION

REPUBLIC OF VIETNAM

Certificate of Excellence

Is Awarded To

BRIGADIER GENERAL ALBIN F IRZYK

Who Displayed An Exceptional Degree Of Proficiency And Devotion To Duty In Support of Military Police Operations In The Saigon/Cholon Area By

Providing us with the resources and command support necessary to be your "strong right arm".

17 November 1967

Date

Gordon D. Rowe

LTC MPC

Commanding

Certificate given to the author by the Commanding Officer of his "right arm," Lt. Col. Gordon D. Rowe.

THE PLAYERS

CHAPTER 13
THE BIG FIVE

Within Saigon, there was located the command, control, leadership, security, governance, and *fate* of the entire country of South Vietnam. The Communist high command was only too well aware of this. That is why they recognized that Saigon was an absolutely necessary prize—militarily, diplomatically, psychologically. If they were able to seize Saigon, they knew that they would have not only the city, but also the entire country by the throat.

There were five elements that together "ran" the country and defended it.

1. Sprawling Tan Son Nhut was without question the best known name and installation in the greater Saigon area, and certainly one of the best known in the country. It was located on the northwest side of Saigon. A portion of the air base was physically adjacent to the MACV complex. The airfield was by far the largest and most important in South Vietnam. The individual in command of the base and commander, as well, of the 7th Air Force was General William M. Momyer. Air Force command and control for all of Vietnam was located at this base. (I had no responsibility for the security or support of the air base.)

2. MACV was United States Military Advisory Command Vietnam. Its commander was COMUSMACV, General William C. Westmoreland. This headquarters, known as MACV, was situated on three acres on the east side of the Tan Son Nhut Air Base. The headquarters was a massive two-story concrete and steel structure with

air conditioned office space for four thousand officers and enlisted staff. (Over four times HAC's total available fighting elements.) Because of its great size and the large number manning the building, it quickly acquired the nickname "Pentagon East." Although HAC was not responsible for the air base, it was fully so for "Pentagon East." The building was included in our real estate "holdings." Similarly, we were responsible for the care and feeding of the four thousand or so who served in the building. MACV was the heart and soul of the entire military effort in South Vietnam.

3. The third most critical and vital American element in Saigon, of course, was the U.S. Embassy. It was a brand new 2.6 million dollar compound. It had just been dedicated and opened three months before. Its six-story chancery building loomed over Saigon like an impregnable fortress. It was a white reinforced concrete complex with a ten-foot wall around it. The building had an outer facade of gleaming white rocket proof concrete and shatterproof Plexiglas windows. The United States ambassador to Vietnam was Ellsworth Bunker. As could be expected, some wag quickly nicknamed the chancery, "Bunker's Bunker." HAC had no responsibility for the Embassy Compound. Its real estate holdings were not included in HAC's real estate inventory. Likewise, HAC had no responsibility for the security of the Embassy. As is the case all over the world where U.S. embassies are located, it had a detachment of U.S. Marines assigned who were responsible for its security. Exterior security, of all things, was the responsibility of the Saigon Police, by then the infamous Canh Sats, who were best known for their corruptness.

4. Joining those three American behemoths was the sprawling Presidential Palace complex. It was here that the president of the Republic ofVietnam resided and from which he governed his country. The president was His Excellency Nguyen Van Thieu. He had been inaugurated as president on October 31, 1967. Thus, he had been on the job, "learning the ropes" for only three months when his country was attacked by the Communists.

5. The Vietnamese Joint General Staff Compound was located one kilometer east of Tan Son Nhut. Within this compound the

South Vietnam military brass and "brains" served, worked, planned, and directed. Of course, HAC had no responsibility for providing any kind of service or support to the Vietnamese.

These were the absolutely top five "players" in the country. They governed South Vietnam and were responsible for and provided for its defense—a country at war. Since the five were clustered tightly in the capital city, there could be no doubt that Saigon was the absolute nerve center for the entire nation. Yet, amazingly, shockingly, unbelievably, incomprehensibly, this city at TET was essentially *defenseless*.

Defenseless? How could that be? If a brilliant individual with great imagination and vision had been assigned the task of preparing a realistic scenario for a war game of the defense of Saigon, his scenario would not have come anywhere close to what actually unfolded. He just could not have anticipated the totally unexpected factors and circumstances that presented themselves at the time and in that way and prevailed.

Despite all the increasing, troubling enemy rumblings out there, why would General Westmoreland, as late as December 15, 1967, turn over and abdicate responsibility for the defense of Saigon to the ARVN? Why would President Thieu, who on that date had been in office but a month and a half, accept that responsibility? Surely, he also must have been aware of the troubling reports of enemy activity.

Because of such reports, military leaders had to concede that the enemy was capable of and might already have decided to take some sort of action. However, it is safe to say that it never crossed anyone's mind, was not a consideration, that the action to be taken would be an attack on Saigon during the one great big, sacred, holy, holiday—TET. After all, there had been but one military action during TET in all of the nation's history. That occurred way back in 1789, when Vietnamese patriots attacked the Chinese in Hanoi. An attack on TET that would pit Vietnamese against Vietnamese on their super holiday was just out of the question. For it to happen would be a monumental, unforgivable sacrilege. No, such an action just could not happen.

So as they had for many decades, Vietnamese soldiers with proper authorization left their posts to join their families. The bulk of the Vietnamese army would be scattered in villages, towns, and cities throughout the country. Those left behind were token forces, a "presence." Garrisons were very lightly manned. The individuals "present for duty" would much rather have been home with their families. The last thing they ever expected and could not possibly imagine was to be called to combat, to face an attacking enemy. So it is understandable that missing was heart, dedication, and the ardent desire to fight for their endangered country.

On January 31, 1968, there were many thousands of American combat troops deployed throughout South Vietnam. Spread out in all directions were corps, divisions, brigades, battalions. Yet, there was not a single American combat battalion in Saigon.

Bottom line after noting these factors and considerations: Saigon at TET was, indeed, defenseless. That is why General Tran Do believed that the city would quickly be his, especially since there could *not be an immediate* American reaction.

THE PLAYERS

CHAPTER 14
THE ENEMY

The attack on Saigon and environs was commanded by Major General Tran Do of the Central Office for South Vietnam (COSVN), the Communist high command for the Saigon area.

It was learned after TET that General Do's command post, from which he controlled the entire Saigon operation, was entrenched in tunnels and bunkers in a cemetery adjacent to the Phu Lain Pagoda, only three kilometers west of the racetrack in a rice paddy fringe of Saigon.

General Do employed a regiment of VC whose mission was to attack and seize Tan Son Nhut. Additionally, he used eleven battalions of over four thousand VC, plus sappers, in his initial attack on Saigon. The eleven-battalion assault force included units familiar with routes into the capital.

General Do's plan called for his elements to capture certain key installations in the city during the night. The eleven battalions would operate under the control of the 9th VC Division. The VC were determined to seize those important Vietnamese and American installations, and to kill all who stood in their way. Once they seized their assigned objectives, they would hold all they had seized, until joined by a second wave of main force units that would arrive at daybreak. Those would quickly brush aside what remained of the resisting ARVN elements, and destroy the Saigon government. That would ignite the people to rise up with and join the liberation fighters. According to their calculations, it would all be over very quickly, with the VC in complete control of the capital *before the U.S. could respond.* A very tidy, neat, and simple operation.

From the early log entries already described, it would appear that General Do's strategy was to spread his forces widely in small groups, and to have a multitude of attacks in an effort to cause maximum confusion, fear and chaos over an extensive portion of the city. For attacks on what he deemed to be especially key installations, he used larger but still very modest groups of forces. Except for the U.S. Embassy, it would turn out that his key targets were mainly South Vietnamese facilities.

Because of the absence of any serious ARVN resistance, the VC were able to capture quickly the ARVN armor and artillery schools. These were supposedly prize objectives because they were expected to provide the VC with the quick use of heavy offensive military equipment that they had been unable to pre-position. They were shocked and dismayed to find no tanks at the armor school, and only damaged and unusable howitzers at the artillery school.

Another severe disappointment: they quickly seized the government radio station. They considered that installation to be vital and critical, for it would enable them to broadcast tapes proclaiming the general uprising. To their great surprise and astonishment, they learned after seizing the installation that the power had been shut off and was unusable. Frustration upon frustration. Three quick victories—seizure of three vital, critical installations, and absolutely nothing to show for it.

While all this was unfolding, there came another crushing blow—this time a staggering defeat. The two biggest, most impressive, most formidable, and most symbolic targets in Saigon were the U.S. Embassy and the Presidential Palace. While a group of sappers attacked the U.S. Embassy, a second group of sappers attacked the Presidential Palace. That is when the ARVN briefly came alive. That installation was by far the most heavily guarded in all of Saigon. The VC obviously miscalculated the resistance that they would receive, for the number in the sapper group was far too few for the task that was assigned to them. The members of the group were quickly cornered and eliminated.

As it would turn out, the VC were guilty of not selecting other important key installations and zeroing in on them with substantial, organized forces.

When daylight came to Saigon, it was clearly and readily apparent that General Tran Do's plan had *failed! The capital was not firmly under the control of the Viet Cong.*

Why?

The VC received two immediate, serious and unexpected jolts that completely upset their careful and extremely optimistic plan.

First, the people were not ignited, and did not rise up. They were still tucked away tightly, out of sight in their homes.

Second, and most importantly and most critically, the U.S. response, which was to be too little and too late, was instead immediate, instantaneous. It was the United States Army Headquarters Area Command (HAC) that did the responding. Its Military Police assumed without delay its secondary mission, "To fight as infantry when required." And they were desperately "required." They were supported by hastily organized reaction forces from HAC resources.

It was perfectly obvious that General Tran Do had been "blindsided" by HAC.

He must certainly have been well aware of General Westmoreland's agreement to give responsibility for the defense of Saigon to the ARVN. He, like everyone else, knew that because of TET, the ARVN strength in Saigon would be low. He also expected that for those "present for duty" the readiness and eagerness to fight would be extremely limited. He was absolutely right. During the early hours of the action, the ARVN was all but invisible. Unquestionably, they were shocked, shaken, and frightened by what was happening out there. Nothing like this was supposed to happen at TET. Moreover, many of the soldiers may have held back, believing that a coup was taking place, and they did not know where and how they fit in. Thus, with greatly diminished and ineffective ARVN forces, and no American troops to be concerned with, he must have figured that it would be a "cakewalk."

But he made a tragic, disastrous mistake. Perhaps he was unaware of the existence of HAC. Or, he may have known of it as a service element that was no threat. For whatever reason HAC was disregarded, ignored. And it was that command that was the bolt that hit him "out of the blue." When the chips were finally counted they revealed that HAC was the prime factor and key reason why General Tran Do's plan had failed.

Had he been acutely aware of HAC, he would have known that for his plan to succeed, it was vital for him to seize and control three HAC elements.

First, General Tran Do should have immediately eliminated the Provost Marshal Compound in downtown Saigon instead of fiddling away time and resources at such places as the armor and artillery schools. The Provost Marshal Compound was HAC's nerve center. This element was as close as HAC could come to having a tactical headquarters. By quickly attacking it, equipped with its military police net control, General Do would have neutralized HAC's eyes, ears, and arms, and wiped out instantly any chance that HAC would have to conduct any kind of coordinated operation in Saigon.

Second, similarly, he should have immediately eliminated the headquarters of the 716th Military Police Battalion and the large International Hotel, with its multitude of military police resources and people. Without that headquarters there would be no one to control the hundreds of MPs and attachments. There would have been no source capable of planning for the employment of the troops, dispatching them and fighting them, which included the organization and deployment of the reaction forces.

General Tran Do's badly missed *third* target, of course, was HAC headquarters This element had, most importantly, operational command of both the 716th and the Provost Marshal. On top of that, it was like an octopus, with its many arms and responsibilities reaching out to all parts of Saigon and Cholon. It did not have the radio capability of the Provost Marshal, but it had an immense telephone network. The headquarters was capable of reaching every billet, every dining facility, every American element, key Vietnamese offices, and every foreign element in its area of responsibility. The seizure of this huge umbrella over Saigon/Cholon would have been a very juicy and essential plum for General Tran Do.

Without these three components, who would it have been that was capable of meeting head on the surprising and very broad Viet Cong attack, blunting them, delaying them, and preventing them from accomplishing their mission? The answer, of course, is no one.

If General Tran Do had quickly eliminated or neutralized those three elements, the battle for Saigon would have ended suddenly, abruptly and most triumphantly for him. The incoming American tactical troops would have found extensive casualties, a totally chaotic city. That undoubtedly, would have required many troops and a prolonged period of house-to-house fighting in order to regain control of Saigon. It would have been an American disaster.

Yes, when Major General Tran Do reached for the "key to the city," HAC yanked it away.

THE PLAYERS

CHAPTER 15
THE MILITARY POLICE

It took the 716th Military Police Battalion less than three hours to transform itself from a police element to one that was as close as it could be to an infantry battalion. It was ready for combat.

The 716th in Saigon/Cholon had an area of responsibility for fifty square miles, within which was included 450 American installations of every size, shape and description—from BOQs and BEQs to warehouses. Because of this, it had become, as stated, the largest MP battalion in the U.S. Army, worldwide. It had recently been augmented by the attachment to it of the 527th Military Police Company. We at HAC had a Security Guard Company of two hundred men. Because of the similarity of missions, I had placed this unit under the operational command of the 716th. Thus the augmented and reinforced battalion was now an increasingly potent force, and would serve as HAC's fighting element. It became my combat arm.

Also assisting the 716th in maintaining their day-to-day security posture was a sizeable number ofVietnamese civilians who had been hired and trained as security guards. Their training included familiarization with small arms weapons. They were armed and were positioned and stood guard at billets and other key HAC installations. Although relatively small in number, these guards provided yet another layer of security.

There was one other defensive precaution that we took. Each hotel and important installation had a defense plan, and had been issued small arms and ammunition. These were controlled by designated, responsible occupants of the installation to be used in case of emergency, or if "all hell broke loose." This, of course, is exactly what did happen during the TET attack. There were many instances when individuals did grab the arms and helped defend their installations. Such unexpected reactions further frustrated the VC.

When the MPs went to bed on the night of January 30th, they were all well aware that something soon could be happening. They were reconciled to the high degree of probability that it would again be isolated terrorist activity. None of them ever *imagined or envisioned the magnitude of the attack that would come.*

The moment he was awake, each man instantly believed the expected terrorist activity was taking place. At first blush, it did appear to each that it was the predictable attacks to which he had on occasion responded. But in almost an instant all came to the grim realization that what was now happening was vastly different, that this activity was of epic proportions—something big, immense that they had not experienced before.

In no time they were out there, moving in all directions. The challenges that faced the 716th were immense. They would instantly be engaged in an unbelievably wide variety of activities. Those activities ran a very broad, extremely varied and totally unprecedented gamut. They had to take head-on the VC, which they immediately encountered. They established and held blocking positions to blunt attacking VC, ran dangerous and lonely jeep patrols in Cholon, conducted rescue missions of billets under siege, undertook reconnaissance missions to detect the location and strength of VC forces, maintained static guard posts at vitally important U.S. installations that were threatened. As part of hastily formed reaction forces, they raced to especially dangerous trouble spots, responded to scores of desperate calls for immediate assistance, often from totally unexpected locations, many coming from places for which they had not been assigned responsibility, such as two hotels used by female employees of the U.S. Agency for International Development, and civilians cut off in VC-held sections of the city.

Before daybreak, more than eight hundred men of the 716th

were in action, and many of those had been in action from the outset. By daylight a significant number had already been killed and wounded. Many brushed aside orders to rest, and would stay in action continuously for more than forty-eight hours. They were disappointed and somewhat handicapped because of the three hundred Vietnamese who normally rode with MP patrols or stood guard at U.S. installations, only twenty-five had reported for duty.

Two decisions made early on paid off handsomely. The boosting of the jeep patrols to forty-one was invaluable in broadening greatly the coverage of the Saigon area. The doubling of many static guard posts was instrumental in discouraging or thwarting VC aggressive intentions.

The MPs had one very significant and important advantage over the VC. They had excellent communications. This was provided by their effective two-way radios. Conversely, the VC operated in small groups with virtually no communications. They had received their assigned missions and orders and off they went. They were tied to the directives issued and missions assigned, and operated rigidly without flexibility. They were not able to report to their higher command their progress or difficulties they encountered. They could not adjust their actions unless forced by the MPs. There was no chance of applying initiative. There was no one for them to contact about changing or modifying their instructions. The higher command was, likewise, handicapped. Without minute-by-minute reports from their attacking elements, they were virtually in the dark about progress of their operations. There was no way that they were able to exert any control, if it was needed. All in all, a tremendous plus for our side.

Although Vietnamese police stations and military installations were located near the biggest battles in the city, the MPs received absolutely no assistance of any kind from them for upwards of the first eighteen hours.

During the battle for the U.S. Embassy, the headquarters of the 1st Police Precinct was next to the Embassy, yet not one of its men joined in the Embassy battle. Even worse and more difficult to accept, during the very costly fights at BOQ #3 and the racetrack, jittery ARVN soldiers fired on our forces in the confusion of the night battles. None left their compounds to join reaction or rescue teams dispatched by the 716th.

The 716th, along with the limited number of armed troopers that HAC was able to provide, fought desperate, lonely, costly delaying actions for many hours. Lonely it was, for the battalion was not part of any regiment, brigade, not part of a division—it was the sole battalion in town, a truly independent battalion. Those MPs were at the forefront of the defense of Saigon, during the first, most critical seventy-two hours.

Captured Viet Cong fighters universally claimed that no matter where they moved, instead of meeting ARVN soldiers, which they expected, they confronted MPs, who seemed to be everywhere. Similarly, the MPs declared that because of the broad and extensive deployment of the VC, no matter which way they moved, they ran into and surprised the VC, who seemed astonished at their presence.

The battle for Saigon was undoubtedly the largest, most extensive, independent military police combat operation in the long history of the Military Police Corps. Had it not been for the actions of the MPs who took the VC head on, the casualties in the city could have been staggering. The intensity of their efforts are revealed by the casualties they suffered. Within the first twelve hours, they had twenty-seven killed and forty-four wounded. During the very early hours, the VC with their rockets, Claymore mines, and satchel charges, destroyed three two-and-a-half ton trucks and more than a dozen jeeps.

For their heroic actions, the 716th Military Police Battalion, with its attached 527th Military Police Company, as well as the 90th Military Police Detachment, would be awarded the Presidential Unit Citation.

Individual awards would include one Distinguished Service Cross, two Silver Stars, eighty-nine Bronze Stars, seventy-one Purple Hearts, and sixty-four Army Commendation Medals.

The history of the U.S. Army Police Corps includes many proud chapters. But there are none that anywhere near compare with the most distinguished performance of the military police in Saigon during the TET offensive of 1968. That chapter will always remain unique, incomparable, and brimming with glory.

Combat MPs.

Typical two-man MP patrol.

MP reaction force formed and ready to mount up.

Ambassador Ellsworth Bunker and General William C. Westmoreland attend a memorial service for the military policemen and service troops killed in the battle for Saigon.

The author holds a steel helmet worn by a military policeman which was crushed when his truck was destroyed by rockets.

AFTERMATH

CHAPTER 16
AFTERMATH

As has been described, MP and HAC elements were involved in critical standoff situations at BOQ #3, the racetrack, and Gate #10. Most fortuitously, they were effectively "bailed out" by tactical elements from the 1st Division at BOQ #3, 3rd Battalion, 7th Infantry at the racetrack, and elements from the 25th Division at Gate #10.

Except for the 3rd of the 7th, the other units were not *entering*, but passing through Saigon headed for their primary mission. By a stroke of good fortune, the passage of those units brought them close to those critical situations. Elements were briefly "sidetracked" and during the brief time available to them were able to turn around three difficult situations. Those actions, however, highlighted what would prove to be a great irony. Astonishingly, what has just been described was the sum total of the support received by HAC within the city of Saigon from the tactical units that began flooding into the Saigon area, eventually thirteen battalions of them.

One report had some of the early battalions in the following locations by February 3:

1. 2/27th Infantry and 3/4 Cavalry (25th Division) were securing the Tan Son Nhut Air Base area.

2. 3/7th Infantry (199th Light Infantry Brigade) was securing the Phu Tho Racetrack area.

3. 2/16th Infantry and A/1/4th Cavalry (1st Division) were securing the Binh Loi Bridge in Northern Saigon.

4. 1/18th Infantry (1st Division) was securing the power plant and water plant east of Saigon.

5. 2/327th Infantry (101st Airborne Division) was securing the POL storage area.

6. 5/60th Mechanized Infantry (9th Division) at Binh Chanh, and the 1/27 Infantry (25th Division) at Hoc Mon were screening the southern and western approaches to Saigon.

Remarkably, this listing does not show, with the exception of the 3rd of the 7th, a single tactical battalion within the city of Saigon committed to helping secure the capital. Moreover, there would be none.

Then soon came a truly unexpected, astonishing development. With the threat to the city gradually abating, the ARVN would suddenly come to life. The Capital Military District (CMD), which controlled the ARVN forces in Saigon, seemingly out of nowhere, "boldly" decreed that it would now assume the responsibility of solely clearing and cleaning out all enemy forces in the city.

The ARVN had apparently belatedly recognized that they had been embarrassed by their almost complete "no show" during the early, critical, and most difficult hours in the fight for their city, the responsibility for the defense of which they had asked for and accepted on December 15, 1967.

It was perfectly evident that they badly wanted to redeem themselves and their reputations by tackling the job alone. They now believed that it was urgent for them to make the necessary effort to prove to the world that they were strong enough to win their capital back, without any more help from their American partners. To do the job the ARVN committed five ranger, five Marine, and five airborne battalions. (Where had they been earlier?) Taken at face value, that seems a most potent force. Yet because of very generous TET leaves, those battalions could not have been at more than a third of their strength. If this was so, the strength of the force would be sifted down to about the equivalent of five ARVN battalions—not really a potent force.

The CMD, in order to ensure primacy in this effort, requested that between February 4 and 5 whatever U.S. tactical forces were in the capital were to be shifted out.

The 3rd Battalion, 7th Infantry on the outskirts of the city at the Phu Tho Racetrack, was the only American tactical unit then in town. As requested, it turned over its positions and mission to the ARVN, and immediately withdrew to its base at Binh Chanh. Now there were none. Then lo and behold, but not surprisingly, after a few days the situation became too hot for the ARVN, and the 3rd of the 7th *was requested to return to finish off the job*, which it did.

Unbelievably, as they planned and considered their decisions and moves, not a single overture to HAC was made by the CMD. At no time did they contact, inform, or coordinate with the HAC headquarters. How insensitive, ungrateful, and unprofessional. Apparently they just did not have the guts to face up to that small, unheralded service element that had carried their fight for them.

After about three and a half days, there were no longer any organized enemy attacks in the city. They had "shot their wad." There was no longer a cohesive enemy force now operating. The VC remaining in Saigon were scattered. No longer would they be operating as a military force, but rather would fight as terrorists or guerillas. Major General Tran Do's plan had failed. COSVN, the Communist high command, clearly recognized this, *[for they made absolutely no attempt to commit the planned and poised second wave of main force units.]* It was clear to them that this was not the time to reinforce failure.

So now Saigon was no longer a combat zone, but continued to be a very dangerous area. The VC scattered around the city would be operating singly, in pairs, and in very small groups. They would hide, pop up at an opportune time and place, fire their weapons, scoot away, and pop up again. They wanted to be a nuisance, and became a deadly one; they harassed, tried to sabotage and kill. HAC's many facilities and its many people were still threatened and vulnerable. Certain BOQ and BEQ hotels were still receiving during the day and at night sporadic bursts of small arms and automatic fire. The VC were particularly active on and about the streets of the city, of which there was a vast network. Consequently, all movement was hazardous—from billet to workplace, to mess facilities, back to billet. There was now no war in Saigon, but it was still a very dangerous place, but would be progressively less so as the VC were eliminated by ones and twos.

HAC's greatest challenges and achievements occurred during the TET attack on Saigon. Its combat demands have already been discussed in considerable detail.

What has hardly been recognized, noted, or commented upon is the second part of the HAC story. As soon as it was clearly evident that the VC mission in Saigon had failed, it was time for HAC to "pick up the pieces," roll up its sleeves, and assume its primary responsibilities of feeding, securing, transporting, maintaining, and housing thousands of people. It was essential to try as quickly as possible to get back to normal while operating under absolutely abnormal conditions.

Even though ARVN elements would be operating in the city, HAC's Military Police would resume its law and order responsibilities. The 716th would gradually, as enemy activities slackened, move from its infantry mode to its Military Police role. But for a time, with scattered armed enemy still out there, they would remain in flak jackets, and with steel helmets and loaded weapons.

For HAC to get on with its job, it had to get its people back to their assigned positions. For this to happen the reaction forces had to be disbanded quickly. Then HAC's "combat elements" could return to being clerks, finance specialists, mess sergeants, housing managers, utility supervisors, motor pool commanders, and a whole host of other responsible jobs. What is absolutely without precedent, and can only be imagined, is that every single individual assigned to HAC, except those individuals who were absolutely and critically essential to running a headquarters under combat conditions, had donned combat gear and had participated in combat missions. As they turned in their flak jackets, steel helmets, weapons and ammunition, one can only wonder and conjecture about the flood of emotions that must have swept over them, as they returned to their primary jobs. None of those individuals, until some hours before, had held a military weapon in their hands since basic training, during their first eight weeks in the army. Now some hours later, they had been shooting at dangerous people, who in turn were firing at them. They had been in very tight spots, life-threatening situations, where it had been touch and go. They watched as comrades were wounded and some killed. Some among them had also been wounded, and some would be decorated for valor. Was all this just a fanciful dream? No! Could it really have happened to them? Yes! But they would never be the same again. They had been tested in combat, among the toughest testing grounds known to man, and had proved themselves. They could now stand tall. What they had experienced would without question be one of the proudest and most defining periods of their lives. During the years ahead, they would surely, many times, relive those moments.

In attempting to return to normal, HAC was faced initially with two extremely significant obstacles and handicaps. The first was the difficulty of movement for individuals and vehicles because of the VC presence. Second was the initial absence, the "no show" of the 6500 loyal, faithful, trained, competent Vietnamese workers who made it possible for HAC to accomplish its many, varied, essential missions. They were slow in emerging from the safety of their homes. However, as soon as these Saigon natives recognized that there was no longer a political threat, no sign of a coup or an uprising and as the ranks of the VC began thinning out, the Vietnamese workers gradually began to return to work. Once they were assured that they, as Vietnamese, were able to make it through the streets of Saigon more easily and safely than Americans, their return to work accelerated, and almost all were finally back.

Until that happened, it was really very tough going for HAC. At the dining facilities, for example, mess sergeants and cooks without help endeavored to prepare meals that many people for so many hours had to miss. At the outset, these meals of necessity were catch as catch can. The mess sergeants did not know what their rations would be and when they would receive them.

Trucks had to negotiate the dangerous streets to reach the ration supply points in warehouses along the Saigon waterfront. On one occasion early on, the trucks had nearly reached the supply point when they were stopped by a firefight up ahead with ARVN on one side of the street and VC on the other, and had to turn back. On another trip a truck was already backing up, ready to begin drawing rations, when automatic fire broke out just outside the compound. And at the insistence of the ration man, the truck quickly disengaged, and dashed back through the gate. It did so safely, for MPs outside the gate had engaged, and were rolling back the VC. In both instances, however, the trucks returned empty-handed, which, of course, was of no help to the mess sergeants.

There were many instances where residents had been cooped up in their hotel rooms since the attack on Saigon began. They desperately wanted to be out. Now, however, the VC, with AK-47s, had posted themselves so as to make it dangerous for residents to attempt to come or go. There was not sufficient weaponry in the hotels to take on the VC. HAC recognized the urgent need to free the hotel inhabitants. As soon as it could, it informed the residents of a hotel that a bus would be by to pick them up, and gave them the time. They were told to carry a minimum amount of personal belongings, and to be ready to rush into the bus the moment it arrived, so that it could move out without delay. Armed MPs would precede and escort the bus. When the time came, and the bus was loaded and moved out quickly and safely, emotional and vastly relieved inhabitants grinned and some tears were shed.

There was one bright, totally unexpected, redeeming factor. It has happened over and over. When a community is in distress, the very best in people comes out; they rise to the occasion. Such happened in Saigon. American civilians from a variety of agencies recognized HAC's problems, volunteered to do something about it, and to help out as best they could. Of all things, some chose the very hazardous job of riding shotgun atop trucks, guarding them as they made their way to the ration points. This was reminiscent of individuals mounted on stagecoaches, guarding gold shipments in old Western movies.

American civilians reported to motor pools and volunteered to drive transport vehicles guarded by MPs, and were able to move significant numbers of individuals to their necessary destinations. Those with culinary knowledge and interest volunteered their services at dining facilities to assist cooks and mess sergeants. Many individuals who for weeks and weeks had been "customers," patrons, and had been served *by* HAC, took off their jackets and ties, moved food from the kitchens to the serving line, and served *for* HAC.

Those individuals collectively undertook an extensive number of tasks that provided an unexpected, most effective and extremely welcome augmentation to the heavily overburdened HAC personnel.

But in the long run, it was the small HAC nucleus, the former reaction force members, who during those early hours kept the engine running. Many of those who normally worked in a supervisory capacity had to shoulder additional jobs, which forced upon them long days and long nights.

The 716th MP Battalion did yeoman work in freeing from their billets hundreds of beleaguered residents. They continued to escort key individuals to their places of duty, and provided armed guards to escort HAC convoys, which had to move back and forth across the city, still under sporadic hostile fire. Thus, HAC was able to gradually and progressively assume its full responsibilities.

The VC, which had infiltrated or invaded Saigon with so much hope and such high expectations on January 31, were either killed or had vanished by February 15. By that date Saigon was back to normal. Or was it? No, it would never be the same. As a wartime city, it now bore such new labels as frightened, chastened, and sobered.

AFTERMATH

CHAPTER 17
OBSERVATIONS/CONCLUSIONS

Top-level American personnel on the ground, when discussing the events in Saigon during TET of 1968, declared that if it had not been for the actions of the United States Army Headquarters Area Command (USAHAC), the VC would have taken over the city.

Seasoned observers after TET: "United States Army Headquarters Area Command saved Saigon."

Major General Tran Do was right when he predicted that he would not have to fight the ARVN when he assaulted Saigon.

Major General Tran Do was wrong when he predicted that people in Saigon were itching to be rid of the "imperialist Americans," and would rise up and welcome the invaders with wide-open arms.

Major Tran Do erred badly. By trying to attack all over town at once, he fragmented his forces. This enabled the small, limited, diverse, lightly armed MPs and HAC reaction forces to "hang in there" successfully.

In the days leading up to TET, Lieutenant General Frederick Weyand, commanding II Field Force, Vietnam, became convinced that the enemy was about to strike the cities of South Vietnam. Radio intercepts had begun to pick up the movement of enemy units toward Saigon. He vehemently and then successfully urged General Westmoreland to redeploy significant numbers of American troops close to and oriented toward Saigon.

If not for the ready availability and quick deployment of these units (brought back from the Cambodian border), it would been a totally different fight for Saigon. The Communist second wave main force would have overwhelmed and engulfed HAC's MPs and reaction forces. The great fight put up by HAC would have been in vain, all for naught. The security force at Tan Son Nhut would have quickly cracked. The tardiness of American reinforcements would have enabled the VC, who in the past had already proven their tenacity, to dig in and prepare a fanatical defense. Late arriving Americans would have had house-to-house fighting over a vast city that would have dragged on, demolishing much of Saigon, but more importantly would have resulted in massive casualties.

That did not happen largely because of the perceptiveness and determination of Lieutenant General Frederick Weyand, who proved to be a dominating factor in saving Saigon.

Enigma: totally, completely, mystifying. During the afternoon and late into the evening on January 30, Saigon was an unbelievably riotous and boisterous city filled with revelers. The streets were so jammed that people could barely move. The celebrating was totally, unabashedly uninhibited. Less than three hours later, the streets were completely empty; cars, motorbikes, bicycles, and people had, somehow, completely vanished. Not a single light was showing; absolutely nothing was moving. It was as though three million people were simultaneously pricked by the bad witch's needle, and life immediately stopped for them. Was there ever before such a complete and radical transformation of such a huge city in such a brief period of time? Totally unrestrained one moment, and totally invisible the next.

The residents of Saigon must have known for some time that "something was up." They had to be aware that weapons were being smuggled in and stashed away. Neighborhoods were tight-knit, had their own underground. They must have known that strangers had slipped into homes in their neighborhoods. Some may have been pressured to rise up; others pressured not to.

So, they must have "known," but how much? What, when, how big?

Then came noise, explosions. As if a single switch were pulled, revelry instantly stopped, and all residents somehow *knew* that it was an attack, that every single individual *had* to rush home, shut himself in, and not to appear. Truly, truly amazing.

Could the "word," like some red, hot juicy rumor, have swept through the streets and underground during the days immediately preceding TET? Did they know that it would be *at* TET?

A tantalizing mystery still.

★ ★ ★

General Westmoreland's Thank You Note to HAC

Headquarter United States Military Assistance Command, Vietnam

26 March 1968

SUBJECT: Commendation

TO: Deputy Commanding General

United States Army, Vietnam

APO 96375

(Italics below are the author's.)

1. I welcome this opportunity to commend the U.S. Army Headquarters Area Command for the outstanding *support* rendered during the recent VC/NVA TET offensive. The magnificent *support provided the COMBAT forces operating in Saigon*, and the successful self-defense of several key military installations is truly *noteworthy*. Individually and collectively, the contributions by personnel of USAHAC to the defeat and destruction of the enemy was marked by selfless determination to maintain security and to provide required *support*, regardless of the obstacles encountered.

2. Please extend my sincere appreciation to the officers and men of Headquarters Area Command for their dedicated *contributions*.

s/W.C. Westmoreland

W.C. Westmoreland

General, United States Army Commanding

(Apparently, there was limited awareness by COMUSMACV and his MACV staff of what actually transpired in Saigon.)

★ ★ ★

In 1968, Saigon was not just another city. It was the capital, the seat of the nation's government. Similarly, the U.S. Embassy was not just another embassy; it was an exceptionally big prize. Had the Viet Cong, during those quick, early hours captured the Embassy, they would have signaled to the Vietnamese, the American people, and to the whole wide world that they were in control of that great symbol of the "imperialist power" of America. That would have gained for the Communists a devastating, powerful victory. The country-wide attacks of which Saigon was the primary target left little doubt that a conclusive phase of the war had begun.

Today there is no Saigon, no U.S. Embassy, only a Ho Chi Minh City.

★ ★ ★

The following is an article written by Robert Stone for the *New York Times*. It was written in 1995, 27 years after the TET Assault. Robert Stone's novel about the Vietnam War, *Dog Soldiers*, won a National Book Award in 1975.

Tet '95—Neither sadder nor wiser

Vhat would it be like to valk around town with Spc. Daniel and Pfc. Sebast 27 years after hey were killed? Surely, hey would have thought ve had won the war.

y ROBERT STONE

On the night of Jan. 31, 1968, a young Vietnamese peasant named Nguyen Van Sau sat with bout 20 companions in a garage not far rom the center of Saigon.

It was the night after Tet, the lunar ew year, and although Communist at- acks the night before had caused the Tet ease-fire to be canceled, the city was full of visitors celebrating the holiday.

Sau and his friends had come to town arrying holiday packages. But Nguyen Van Sau and the others were not in Saigon to celebrate. They were members of Sapper Battalion C-10 of the Viet Cong, and their packages were weapons.

Sau had grown up just outside the capital. In the National Liberation Front, he had learned to read and write. As a special honor, he was invited to join the Communist Party. And now he had been singled out again. The men and women of Sapper Battalion C-10 were going to attack the United States Embassy.

At around 2:45 a.m., their little convoy set out in an old Peugeot van and a taxi of the same make, both familiar vehicles on Saigon streets.

At 3 a.m., the guerrillas in the taxi opened fire on the military police post at the embassy's entrance. The MPs returned fire and slammed shut and locked the steel gate. The Viet Cong used an antitank explosive to breach the wall.

In seconds, a commando squad of about two dozen was pouring through it. The two MPs turned to face them. The first American to die was Specialist 4 Charles L. Daniel of Durham, N.C. He and his partner, Pfc. William Sebast of Albany, fell defending their positions, and their refusal to yield or withdraw probably spoiled the attack.

The battle for the embassy grounds went on through the night. By 9 a.m., all of the attackers had been killed or captured. The American dead consisted of the two MPs and one Marine. The Communists had failed to gain entrance to a single building.

1993 FILE PHOTO

A cyclo driver carries color TV sets to an electronics shop in Hanoi.

Up until that point in the war, nearly 20,000 Americans had died along with hundreds of thousands of Vietnamese. More than 58,000 Americans and an estimated 4 million Vietnamese would die before it was over.

During the early hours of Jan. 31, 1968, there was fierce fighting in Saigon and all over Vietnam. But the attack on the embassy was perhaps the engagement that most fascinated the world.

In January, I spent a few days in Saigon, now called Ho Chi Minh City. It was coming up on Tet, and everyone was buying presents.

The town was booming as never before. Foreign businessmen, including plenty of Americans, were everywhere.

On the roof of the Rex, the hotel that once was the American bachelor officers' quarters, tourists and local plutocrats were dining on frogs' legs.

Diners at the Rex can watch the streets below illuminated by Toshiba and Sony neon signs that turn night into day.

On what was the Rue Catinat before it was Dong Khoi Street, antique porcelain and jewelry are for sale.

What would it be like to walk around town with Spc. Daniel, Pfc. Sebast and Nguyen Van Sau and his comrades of C-10 one of these lovely holiday evenings, 27 years after the attack that killed them?

Would they guess who had won the war in which they died? Surely, the Americans would have thought it was their side. And Sau might be amazed at the fruits of the Communists' victory.

Dong Khoi, the street where you get the antique jewelry and porcelain, means Spontaneous Uprising — presumably the one Sau and his friends waited all night in vain for in 1968.

Although the uprising never came, they changed the street name anyhow.

Today, many a deal is in the making. In Hanoi and Ho Chi Minh City, new factories will soon make Wisk liquid soap and Sunlight detergent for the Vietnamese kitchen. And before long, there will be a new U.S. embassy in Hanoi.

How ironic it all is. Perhaps such a squandering of young lives ought to be consigned to the realm of private grief.

Yet we find ourselves moved and inspired by the heroism of young people who do their duty, who serve with all the vigor of their youth, strength and courage. The political futility of their sacrifice gives it a poignancy.

After a period of denial and ambiguity, the United States began erecting fitting monuments to the Americans who died in our futile war.

Somehow we can't keep ourselves from honoring those who give their lives in the wars to which our shortsightedness and folly consign them. Yet we know that in every war lives are lost, meaninglessly, and that the cause behind their sacrifice is soon rendered irrelevant.

We have never succeeded in replacing proper conduct on the field of battle as the ultimate measure of courage and loyalty. We have not developed that "moral equivalent of war" that William James so wisely and impossibly called for.

Knowing not a whit more than the ancient Greeks, we console ourselves as they did in catharsis, in stoic acceptance and tragic ritual. Our celebration of death in battle is, from a certain perspective, utterly irrational.

Yet it is our only means of imposing some degree of meaning on war's meaningless destruction, the only way we have of facing the eternal ironies of history.

■

Robert Stone, whose novel about the Vietnam War, Dog Soldiers, *won a National Book Award in 1975, is also author of* Outerbridge Reach. *He wrote this article for* The New York Times.

New York Times article by Robert Stone about the TET Assault in 1968.

Brigadier General Albin F. Irzyk during the Vietnam era.

ACKNOWLEDGMENTS

This book has been written based on my firsthand knowledge and recollections, and my personal records. Even after forty years, much of what is covered here remains clear and vivid. However, time has a way of dimming details. I was most fortunate to have had the following to "lean on."The assist gained from these sources was most significant, and I am profoundly grateful for it.

Of particular help to me and for which I am especially appreciative is a pamphlet dated March 16, 1983, written by SSG Thomas L. Johnson and Mary R. Himes of the Military Police Corps Regimental Museum, and is entitled "Historical Account of the Military Police Corps Regiment Assault on the American Embassy, TET-1968." I wrote the Foreword and was interviewed for this publication.

Battle for Saigon, Tet 1968, Keith William Nolan. Pocket Books, 1996.

Historical Account of the Military Police Corps Regiment Assault on the American Embassy TET 1968, SSG Thomas L. Johnson and Mary R. Himes. Military Police Corps Regimental Museum, 1983.

"Battleground Saigon," John C. McManus. *Vietnam Magazine*, February 2004.

"Saigon's Fighting MPs," Robert L. Pisor. *Army Magazine*, April 1968.

"Tet in Saigon," Don North. *Vietnam Magazine,* February 2000.

Photos are a very important element in this book. Great risks were taken to produce these pictures. Credit goes to the following:

Specialist Five Edgar Price
First Lieutenant E.B. Herr Neckar of the 69th Signal Battalion (A)
Specialist Five Don Hirst of the U.S. Army Headquarters Area Command